Solitary Confinement

Solitary Confinement

Christopher Burney

Introduction by Ted Gioia
Afterword by Hugh Purcell

RECOVERED BOOKS
BOILER HOUSE PRESS

Contents

3

Introduction
by Ted Gioia

11

Solitary Confinement
by Christopher Burney

163

Afterword
by Hugh Purcell

185

Descent from Ararat
by Christopher Burney

Introduction
by Ted Gioia

How Christopher Burney Discovered Mindfulness in a Nazi Solitary Confinement Cell

Many books have been written about the joys of the contemplative life. But I only know of one written by a prisoner in solitary confinement.

Christopher Burney had it worse than almost any inmate today. Captured by the Nazis in occupied France and held in Fresnes Prison, he survived on a single daily bowl of watery soup with a little bread—and even that was taken away sometimes in punishment.

His tattered blankets offered little protection against the cold. At one point, guards even removed his thin mattress, forcing him to sleep on the stone floor.

But worst of all, Burney constantly feared torture and execution.

Burney had operated as a British agent behind enemy lines, and knew secrets that could endanger the lives of colleagues.

When he heard footsteps outside his cell, he feared that the deadly moment had arrived. Authorities had come to interrogate him with all the brutal tools of their trade.

Survival was unlikely. Once he had told them everything he knew—and how could he avoid it when tortured?—he would certainly be executed for espionage.

This is the setting for Burney's book *Solitary Confinement*, one of the great masterpieces of contemplative literature.

The book has been out of print and hard to find for years. But that tells you more about our narrow pop culture concepts of heroes. They're supposed to fight Nazis like Indiana Jones, with fancy tricks and special effects—not practice mindfulness in a cold, dank cell.

In fact, I've only encountered one serious appraisal of this book, from literary critic Frank Kermode. But he understood how valuable Burney's testimony was. 'The courage and the intellectual integrity of this writer', Kermode declared, 'are far beyond what most of us would expect of ourselves'.

More to the point, Burney gave a stirring example we can learn from today—and without undergoing the risks and stresses of 526 days in an isolation cell.

In the early days of World War II, Burney served as a lieutenant in the British Army before getting enlisted for a dangerous secret mission. He wasn't especially brave or tough, but was recruited for his commando training and, especially, his mastery of French. He spoke the language fluently and idiomatically.

Assigned a new identity as 'Christophe Brunet', Burney parachuted into the French countryside on May 30, 1942. He found his way to Caen in Normandy and tried to rendezvous with the local resistance group, codenamed Autogiro, working to destabilize Nazi supply lines. What he did not know was that it had been infiltrated already by a double agent working for the Germans, Mathilde Carre, and most of its members had been arrested.

Because of her betrayal, the Gestapo tried to arrest Burney almost from the moment he arrived in Caen. But he shrewdly identified the police stakeout at his first appointment with his contact in Autogiro, and went on the run to Paris.

The Nazis pursued him relentlessly. They even sent a warning letter to hotel workers and bank employees, which included a good description of the spy—tall, fair-skinned, and looking very British. With his cover blown, with no other resistance contacts, and with no means to communicate with London, there was no safe place to hide. After a few weeks he was spotted by a clerk whose job was to renew ration cards. She tipped off the Gestapo.

Two plain-clothes Gestapo agents arrested Burney in the early morning of August 15, 1942. He was beaten, interrogated, and then locked up in solitary confinement at Fresnes Prison—where he spent the next 17 months.

Most of our other great works about the contemplative life are written by monks and mystics. But Burney was a young, active man in his mid-20s, and totally unprepared for a life of isolation. He wasn't especially religious or philosophical, and had few intellectual resources to fall back on.

Further interrogations did not begin for several weeks. But hunger and cold threatened to kill him before the Nazis got around to it. He tried to treat his tiny food ration as a three-course meal—but it wasn't easy:

> I took the soup slowly, drinking the water first and eating the questionable solid afterwards, pretending in this way that it was a meal of two courses....
>
> To keep my bread untouched was always difficult, and the more so as time went on and I became chronically hungrier, but I decided that it was the best course. For there were ten hours during the night during which nothing could happen, nothing be done except lie in bed, and to pass them awake and on an empty

stomach was an ordeal which was best avoided....I hid the crust under a blanket, or even under the bed, and tried to convince myself that it was not really there.

The day of interrogation finally arrived, and Burney amazed himself by his ability to construct an intricate series of lies and alibis. He even signed a confession, but it was filled with bogus details.

For a while this kept him alive, but soon authorities higher up the command chain decided he had lied, and brought him in for more questioning. Again he exercised his ingenuity and somehow managed to avoid execution without betraying his friends. He was sent back to Fresnes, but he was always at risk.

The biggest challenge was just filling up the hours while awaiting an uncertain fate.

Burney later claimed that he would have welcomed insanity as a kind of escape. He even tried to lose his wits, but such things are not matters of choice. Instead he stayed coldly rational—and was forced to devise some meaningful daily routine with almost no resources at hand.

I've written elsewhere of the remarkable powers of rhythm and music, which are sadly underappreciated in our society today. We use songs for entertainment and diversion, when they can offer so much more. Burney also came to this realization, but through sheer necessity.

But he wasn't a musician. And there were no songs to hear. So how could he tap into this power?

Burney writes:

I embarked on a musical program to conclude [each] day. Being no singer, even to my own taste, I whistled every tune I could remember, the martial ones to make me triumphant over my enemies, the homely ones which made me think of food, and the emotional ones which occasionally, and to my own amusement, brought a conventional tear out of its duct.

This was a long program which grew as my memory became sharper and it brought me easily to a point where I could say, 'Now it doesn't matter if I do eat my bread.' And, having reached this point, I found it easy to go on almost forever....

Yet this was a risky practice—because music of any sort was forbidden at the prison:

Once or twice my performances were interrupted by the entry of an infuriated sentry. Our regular guards never worried over such details, but the mean substitutes who replaced them at weekends could only use petty excuses to intrude upon us.

But even without music, Burney found tremendous comfort in rhythm.

Like so many prisoners, he resorted to pacing. He didn't have much room to operate, and experimented with different ways of navigating through his 10 by 5 foot cell. At first he thought that walking in a circle would give him a greater 'sense of liberty'— and even pushed his bedding up against the wall to make space for a tiny round pathway. But he finally found that a patterned beat, much like the time signature in a composition, offered the greatest source of relief.

The experiment proved that the most satisfactory method was to go straight up and down, taking five paces from end to end and pivoting round on the last in such a way as to keep the rhythm even. It was strangely calming and absorbing.... The motion and sound became hypnotic, like the drip of water or the pulse of a drum.

He now had a suitable pace. And he also had a kind of clock—really just a moving shadow on the wall, but it allowed him some way of measuring the passage of the day.

But he also needed something to feed his mind.

Anything he could summon from memory was a treasure—a few lines of a poem, a recollection of a good meal, a proverb or literary passage, or some other tidbit from the past. Sometimes he would set himself arbitrary tasks—trying, for example, to list the counties in England and Scotland, or the states in the US. Or he would pick two cities and imagine a journey from one to the other, identifying all the people and places along the way.

But, even better, the guards occasionally gave Burney some scraps of paper. He paid the closest attention to whatever was written on them, even if it seemed useless:

> My paper ration one day produced the last few pages of a book by Sir James Jeans on Planck's Constant, translated into French; and although physics had never reached such a level in my world, I was able after many days of concentration to understand the argument, which, I imagine, was set out for novices.

But over time, Burney managed to reach some higher realm of contemplation. This is perhaps not surprising—philosophers as great as Socrates and Boethius found inspiration while awaiting execution. What makes Burney's case so fascinating is that he was not a trained philosopher or scholar of any sort.

Yet he now embarked on detailed meditations on the great problems of human existence. He explored the paradoxes of free will, the nature of individual responsibility, the dualism of soul and body, and other issues that a philosophy grad student might examine. But in Burney's case, he had no teacher or texts, merely his own intellectual resources and dogged persistence, fueled by the empty hours.

He shares many of his musings in *Solitary Confinement*. Sometimes the results are impressive. For example, he dug deeply into the nature of evil—something that a prisoner held by Nazis would inevitably think about. This issue has bedeviled the greatest minds since the earliest days of rational speculation, and Burney came up with a theory surprisingly close to what Boethius had concluded in his own prison cell back in 523 A.D.

Just as light possesses power, and darkness is merely its extinction, so too does good contain an active energy that evil can never match. On this basis, Burney abandoned the conventional view that good and evil were polar opposites—instead adopting a scale in which 'only positive degrees of good' had meaning and efficacy. This allowed him to accept everything with an embracing mindset of optimism—'the good in life', he declared, 'is no longer overshadowed by its imperfections....The tiniest window bringing light will always dominate the bleak and oppressive walls'.

By the time he reached the end of his stay in Fresnes, Christopher Burney had achieved a state of inner peace he would have hardly thought possible at the outset. These many months of solitary confinement, he eventually decided, were 'an exercise in liberty'. They had allowed him to 'scan the horizon of existence' and he had received glimpses of an enlightenment 'behind the variety and activity of life'. This kind of hard-won serenity would have never been granted him in more comfortable settings.

'Solitude,' he concluded, 'is liberty indeed.'

Perhaps others have reached the same conclusion, in some retreat or hermitage. But few have done so in such a dire situation, and with so many threats hanging over their heads. If mindfulness is possible in those circumstances—with so little to see, touch, hear, or taste—imagine what riches it can offer to us, with the whole world at hand.

卌

Solitary Confinement

by Christopher Burney

卌

To Julia

For no thought is contented. The better sort,
As thoughts of things divine, are intermix'd
With scruples, and do set the word itself
Against the word:
As thus—*Come, little ones*; and then again—
It is as hard to come, as for a camel
To thread the postern of a small needle's eye.
Thoughts tending to ambition, they do plot
Unlikely wonders; how these vain weak nails
May tear a passage through the flinty ribs
Of this hard world, my ragged prison walls;
And, for they cannot, die in their own pride.
Shakespeare, King Richard II, Act V

Preface to
Second Edition

When the publishers of the first edition of this book had read the manuscript they asked me to *end* it. They claimed that to leave myself, as they saw it, in mid-career was to cheat the reader. What had happened afterwards? How had I felt in Buchenwald, which was my next port of call, and after that in the ordinary world as it is supposed to be?

I was obstinate, and the book was published as it stood, but the reasons I gave never convinced them that it ended when the episode of solitary confinement ended, and that even the last few paragraphs were gratuitous embroidery. I was asked to round it off, but there was no round end. But it is inevitable that autobiography can have no end that is really an end, and I think that episodic or anecdotal autobiography may be the nearest to truth, because a man who does not know the end cannot really be entrusted with the artistic process of arranging his episodes into a satisfactory whole picture. Even if he did know the whole truth by some prescience, pride might amend it. Mere self-respect would limit me.

As it happens, the eighteen months of solitude which I compressed into this book are as nearly as I can imagine an integral episode. This was the prime number of my series: nothing that followed it was in any way related to it except by the series. Buchenwald was its noisy, crowded and disgusting opposite, and life since the war, though resonant with Buchenwaldian undertones from time to time, has never thrown up the remotest affinity with my hermitic months in Fresnes. The only man whom I have seen both there and since is almost unrecognisable. This is Edmond Michelet, my neighbour for a few months in 1943 and now, by some kind quirk of justice, *Garde des Sceaux*[1] and head of all the prisons of France. Now he is spruce and shaven and bears his real name, but it is the old, scarcely glimpsed unshaven 'terrorist' called Bernard that I shall always remember first.

This was an *intaglio* among the pencil-drawings of experience, small, acute and durable; and it still seems to me that my original decision was right and that I should make no attempt to prolong the story beyond its abrupt end into the framework of a social existence. But sixteen years have now passed since that end and ten years since I finished writing about it, and at such a distance I can try to compromise with my critics by adding some reflections from the looking-glass of freedom. But they are short, and I will keep them apart in this preface. Nor is there much history in them to satisfy the factually curious, for my life since the war has been of no great consequence. So perhaps, after all, it is no compromise at all but a simple indulgence of my own love of speculation.

There was, of course, no necessity to write at all, but in all animals abnormal experience urges communication. The more stupid the dog the more it barks, and nothing makes for more

---

1   French: Keeper of the Seals, a title from the time of the French monarchy now held by the Minister of Justice.

chatter than ignorance. But I also believe that experience is inter-esting when it throws light on our mysterious condition, and that when evidence is available it should be deposed. It may not come out in court, but there it is if it is wanted. And I suppose, to be honest, one always thinks it urgent, if not vital.

Two questions suggest themselves to me in retrospect: was this evidence reasonably accurate, and does it contribute to any tenable view of life seen from a more everyday position?

As to the first, I answer myself in a qualified affirmative. Apart from the difficulty of precise recall, the main problem in writing this book was to describe an uncommon way of life with-out failing to communicate anything at all, but also without so overstating either the highlights or the hardships—the priceless luxuries and their considerable cost—as to distort the balance of truth. The experience of unpleasantness is as exaggerated in the second-hand reading as it is dimmed in the first-hand remember-ing. The imagination can be fired more readily than the memory, which is why pacifist movements are led by the callow rather than by the battle-weary. And to compensate for this freakishness of the human brain I had to sacrifice something at each extreme, while in any case it was impossible to paint the whole picture intelligibly in all its detail when there was so much total empti-ness between the actions as to make it resemble an astronomer's description of the universe. Some choice was imperative, and to that extent some artifice.

To the second question no direct reply is possible, for to say that all personal views of life are affected by experience is to labour the obvious. Moreover, the object of putting the evidence down is not to fix the conclusions to which it leads but to make it possible for a great number of possible conclusions to be modified. But looking back, I can see one essential aspect of this episode which is not emphasized anywhere in the book but which is implicit throughout. (One percipient reviewer glimpsed it.) This is that the subject was an insulated Anglo-Saxon who subsequently returned to the insulated Anglo-Saxon way of life.

Most people outside the Anglo-Saxon world have political violence in their blood, and with it the necessary antibodies. By political violence I mean everything associated with a mere riot or with foreign occupation, and I am thinking principally of the French because I know them best, though the same can be said with variations of the Italians, Czechs, Poles and even the Germans. Generation by generation they have passed through crisis after crisis, and in the times of peace they do not quite relax, never knowing what upheaval or interference will come tomorrow.

This watchfulness over their personal independence and integrity has grown into their character almost as the rules of equity were grafted onto English law. It is not easy to detect for what it is and can easily be confused with cussedness or incivility or plain rebelliousness. The French themselves describe a mulish character as a 'tête de Breton'.

The Englishman, on the other hand, has for so long been kept at a safe distance from political violence of any consistency that he has lost the character of potential victim and with it his protective colouring. When peace is broken (by foreigners) he goes soberly to war, and if he is taken prisoner he stays in company with his fellows and organises his existence according to the established rules. He never becomes a foreigner. This is the cohesive strength for which we are so envied abroad and which gives us phlegm, tolerance and our rather priggish conservatism.

In two places in this book I refer to my reluctance to correspond with my neighbour in the cell next door. On the first occasion my reason was a good one, since he might easily have been an informer. But on the second it was pure self-sufficiency. I simply could not be bothered to interrupt my own train of thought. Thinking—musing would be a better word—was by this time my whole life outside my appetite, and I can remember to this day how petulant I became about it. Once I had embarked on a train of thought I only wanted to stay on it, and it never occurred to me that my neighbour's desire to talk was no less legitimate than mine to be silent. If I had, no doubt my version of legitimacy would have won.

The French, however, demonstrated that their instinctive resilience in the face of oppression was accompanied by recognition that the common plight constituted an immediate bond. And this was not the loose bond of mutual help or encouragement, but more like an automatic friendship, as if the world of trouble imposed standards of its own in total replacement of those of the world of peace. If camaraderie were still a pure word I could use that, but it has been corrupted, and 'naturalness' is too vague. There was no conformity to a type, because it was taken as implicit that every individual was different except in the role of victim, and tolerance was not of the kind which admits discrepancies but does not wish to acknowledge them, but of the kind which takes oddity as an essential part of life itself. Solidarity, another abused word, sounded at its best through the windows of Fresnes, and to be able to combine solidarity of plight with diversity of state must be the highest achievement of the race.

But the greatest achievements of the human being are only within reach when no more food, no greater warmth or comfort can be achieved by a man's exertions. We were in that state in Fresnes, and when we left it we were truly 'poor in spirit'. Buchenwald put some false notes into the harmony because it gave opportunities for more or less food, harder or easier work, and a slower or quicker death. There every crime was committed and every kindness done, but the essential community, though ragged at the edges, never gave way. For what breaks community is contempt, and contempt with us was never a real feeling but only a verbal expletive.

Wariness of the world and acceptance of persons, hard-headedness and generosity, informal and undisciplined solidarity—these are, I think, the main characteristics of this quality of the political victim—this rootless familiarity—which is so different but so difficult to differentiate from simple community of interest. If the poor stand together, so do the rich—there is more in it than that. But I do not suggest that this relationship is meritorious *per se*, nor that there is any mystical or sentimental bond, which there is not. By its origin it precludes all elegance in the body politic, but at the same time its long absence from England has lost us the use of the second person singular. By the same token, I find it impossible to convey otherwise than by allusion the true nature of what I have been trying to describe.

It may seem strange that I have put this distillation of fellowship in the forefront of the preface to a book on solitude. But it was only the hidden face of the moon. This thin residue of society served to mark solitude for what it was, pointing by contrast to the absence of constraint by other minds on my own musings and to the futility of economic effort.

Solitude is liberty indeed, bounded only by the obsessive appetite and the animal lust to roam. But liberty itself is a rare and refined spirit, so strong that Providence in its wisdom has arranged that there shall be little of it, making men live in a society to which solitude is repugnant. Its dilution by the invisible but constant companionship of an active world made these eighteen months an exercise rather than a transcendence.

Herein perhaps lies implicit the relevance of this episode to the tangled undergrowth of knowledge and ideas upon which ordinary life is set. Experience is ordinarily diffused: we receive it indifferently directly or by transference from others, but assemble it wholesale into a philosophy or such less pretentious view that we may take. Great quantities of data are ingested and put through the wobbly process of our judgment, irrespective of whether they come from our direct perception or from more or less accurate reporting, and emerge at the other end in the form of convictions or of those prejudices and conventions which betray the lack of conviction. Above all, so it goes, we must know where we stand, see reality through unblinkered eyes and, with our knowledge that humanity is imperfect, be forever on our guard against our fellows. My small direct experience leaves me cloudy about reality and convinced only that all these things are nonsense. Down on the bedrock, life becomes a love affair of the mind and reality merely the eternally mysterious beloved. Men are just men like oneself but different, ships plying the same sea and weathering the same storms, to be fended off only when they grapple you and otherwise to be saluted, succoured and respected. All we need is the freedom of this small landlocked sea and our daily bread, and my appreciation of the latter in its most rigid sense is not quite equalled by my mistrust of admirals.

Experiences of such rarity in a lifetime engender some sentiment of privateness which in careless moments can seem paradoxically like nostalgia. It is nothing so affectionate, and if the events in this book were repeated I would certainly go quickly out of my mind. But I would not have them undone, for if I did I would lose that strange and faithful fraternity of the windows and those moments when the mind's eye, like a restless prism, could see reality as no more than an outline against the faintly discerned first light of truth.

C.B.

June 1960

卌

Preface to
First Edition

This book should have been a diary. That form of writing not only palliates the first person singular but has the added convenience of ensuring that afterthought is neither included by the writer nor suspected by the reader. Alternatively, in a book of memoirs afterthought is intended by the writer but severely discounted by the reader. Having written neither the one nor the other—for lack of means at the time and of years later—I must preface the book with a word of definition.

This is an account of what went on during eighteen months of solitary confinement, but not a word of it was, nor could have been, written until some eighteen months after the end of the period. Some of the incidents in the early weeks, therefore, were brooded upon, hoped about and criticized hour after hour in the following months. My account of them I believe to be accurate, but I must admit that cogitation may have tailored them to psychological ends. Having no real means to verify them and eliminate any results of wishful thinking, I can only give the account I think true with this qualification: if there is any bias, it is undoubtedly in the direction of making me cleverer than I really was.

On the other hand, I have been diligent in whittling away all the afterthoughts which I sometimes found creeping in. Since I first began to write, more than six years ago, I have read many books. If I had read them earlier I might have been able to portray here a rather more mature and instructed process of thought than now appears, but it would not have been true to superimpose them afterwards. Statements of belief and judgment are therefore indicative of what I believed then, without regard to what I have since learned. For example, I wonder now whether the guards of the prison do not come very well out of it, although I loathed them at the time. This limitation in time I believe to be essential, though it requires some care: the value of an antedated cheque is always precarious and its negotiation difficult.

I will not embarrass the few friends who read the manuscript by naming them. One caused me to write a preface, another to change a word, while the third simply thought me mad. I am equally grateful for the trouble and perspicacity of each of them and for the pains taken by the publishers.

November, 1951.

卌

Chapter 1

In the headquarters of the Security Police, at the rue des Saussaies in Paris, a guard brought me downstairs from the interrogation room. He slammed and locked the door of a cell and left me surprised; for the cell was light and reasonably clean, not unlike a saddle-room without harness, with khaki blankets thrown across an iron cot, whereas I had expected a traditional oubliette, squalid and dank, with a remote pin-point of light above the dripping walls.

Solitude and confinement were both unreal ideas to me, and if I now said to my sub-conscious self 'You are in prison', it was with the conventional notation of a child reading from a picture book words that he cannot read: 'This is the clock that goes tick-tock'. I could see the walls and be impressed by them, but I could not read the writing. Yet, being shut in this little airy cell was the miniature prelude to what was to become life in a new element, a change as drastic as a transformation of the lungs to use some other gas than oxygen, a rarefaction, seeming often like death, and yet fuller of elemental life than the red-blooded world outside. Had I known that life is the crossing of a series of discreet thresholds to the future instead of believing it to be the continuous unfolding of the consequences of the past, I might have spent my few minutes in this gentle ante-chamber in a more philosophical mood.

But the recent past and the immediate future appeared as a smooth and speedy progress of calamity which would at almost any moment be abruptly ended in finity. The humiliation of arrest, early in the morning in my shirt-tails, my confused inability to escape, the handcuffs, the finger-printing and the short sardonic interrogation seemed like a line of telegraph poles seen from the rear end of a train, dwindling into an earlier infinity where lay peace and security and the daily round.

I felt the sense of impotence, of inexorable subjection to a machine of nameless horror, which Peter Bezukhov felt among the ruins of Moscow. It was useless to think of taking action: there was nothing to fight nor anywhere to go. In due course, depending on how the machine was geared, some unimaginable scene would be enacted and the story would end; and neither I nor my enemies, nor the lock on the door nor the bars on the windows, would direct it. We would be puppets dangling in our allotted roles, twisting and turning to the pressure of unseen hands.

Through the bars of the window I could see a little courtyard of green grass, with a tall tree casting a squat shadow in the sun. Beyond the courtyard was an apartment building, and in a window high up a man was shaving, taunting me for an early worm.

Some charwomen were working in a corridor which ran along the left side of the courtyard. They came to look at me surreptitiously from an open window, whispering among themselves, and I called to them as loudly as I dared that they should remember my name, hoping absurdly that they would gossip and that the news would reach friendly ears. In such a case my few friends would have to turn away and make sure to hide every trace of their connection with me; but it was not for this right and proper purpose that I called, but in the selfish and delirious hope that they would arrange my rescue.

One of them, if I judged the time aright, was waiting for me at a cafe not half a mile from the rue des Saussaies. I had passed it in the police car in the early morning, when it was empty and glistening with the aqueous chiaroscuro of the scrubbed parts of Paris on a fine morning. His name was Sébastien, and he would sit at the back of the terrace, with his tinted glasses, black moustache and reserved expression stamping him as a suspicious character, yet endowed with a respectability which made suspicion seem too simple.

It was to be our last meeting before my departure across the Loire to procure communication for us with the outside world and a new name for myself to replace the one which my too frequent journeys had made conspicuous. I found myself growing impatient at the delay and at my inability to warn him that I would be late.

There was my friend Jacques Fouré, who only last night had obtained some clothes for me which were more suitable than my absurd business suit for a long journey through the country. Finally, there was Madame Terrien, in Caen, from whom I had found a postcard when I returned to my hotel last night and to whom I had written a reply before going to sleep. Those two documents were now upstairs, and their only safeguard was the false name under which I addressed her. All these people were in the greatest danger, but I was not yet conscious of it nor of my responsibility in it, since I could not grasp the finality of my own downfall.

For imagination is an optimist, and I conceived this cell not as a place of incarceration, where the damned were jettisoned, but as a waiting room where suspected innocence was kept while suspicion was removed. Upstairs men were arguing my case, some doubtful whether there could be harm in so poor a fish (those would be the two who had seen me in my shirt-tails), others cautious, preferring to make sure by telephoning to Sancerre, where I claimed to have been born, for confirmation of my papers. There was no question in my mind but that the former would prevail and that in a few minutes the door would be opened and I would be let out into the street again.

The charwomen made helpless, sympathetic gestures, and the door opened. A soldier took me by the arm and led me out to the forecourt of the building, where a prison van was waiting. I was crammed into a compartment, and the van left at once. I tried to follow its course by feeling the turns, but being able to see nothing I was soon lost, and when we stopped again and I was rushed out of the van and into another large building, I had no idea of where I was. I only realised that it was a prison, bleak and uncompromising, boding not temporary detention, but an irrevocable end, where men wait powerless and destitute on 'the crowded, arid margins of existence'.

Two armed soldiers led me down a long, damp tunnel until we emerged on the ground floor of a high, hollow rectangle, with four storeys of cells built into each outer wall and a narrow gangway running round each level, the empty central shaft being crossed with iron bridges. A third soldier received me here and led me to the topmost floor, where a sergeant took away my shoelaces, searched me and gave me a piece of paper, saying, *'Lisez'*. I saw that these were the prison rules, but I did not bother to read them, since I could safely assume that everything was forbidden, and the sergeant, not caring whether I read or not, then said ominously, *'Komm!'* and ushered me into cell No. 449.

The door slammed behind me with a crash, the double lock bolted with two heavy clicks, and I was alone. The numbness which had possessed me since morning was beginning to recede: disaster had heaved and shaken and had now subsided, and I could survey the wreckage with a slow beam of understanding. For the first time since my arrest I acted rationally, if hopelessly, going to the window and door to make sure that no one had been careless. But when I had only done so much I was relieved that I had found no opportunity to do more. I wanted to swear, to jump up and down, to break china. I was petulant but not yet enough persuaded of the truth to be purposeful. Over the truth still lay a mist, as it were of a dream or a stupid joke, and I could neither believe nor wake nor laugh.

I looked again at the window. It was a high French window of opaque panes, firmly locked, and at the top there was a sky-light, which opened by falling thirty degrees backward into the cell. Through the frosted glass I could see nothing but the vague shadow of another building, but in the gap over the open skylight there was framed a small oblong of blue sky. I stared at this sky, trying by gazing to be drawn to it.

A slight sound made me turn. In the middle of the door there was a peep-hole, which had been uncovered. Through it a cold blue eye, like slimy glass, was watching me. I looked vainly at the iron bed, the wooden table hinged to the wall and the stool chained to it, at the thin straw mattress, the ragged blankets and the dirty earthenware toilet in the corner. There was nothing even to throw. Then the shutter of the peep-hole slid back, and the eye disappeared, leaving me sick at heart and angry as a child.

\

Chapter 2

I soon learned that variety is not the spice, but the very stuff of life. We need the constant ebb and flow of wavelets of sensation, thought, perception, action and emotion, lapping on the shore of our consciousness, now here, now there, keeping even our isolation in the ocean of reality, so that we neither encroach nor are encroached upon. If our minds are thus like islands, they are of many shapes, some long and straight, others narrow and bent, a few nicely rounded, and yet others round and hard, impervious to the sea and belching from deep unapproachable cones the universal warmth which lies beneath us all. We are narrow men, twisted men, smooth and nicely rounded men, and poets; but whatever we are, we have our shape, and we preserve it best in the experience of many things.

If the reach of experience is suddenly confined, and we are left with only a little food for thought and feeling, we are apt to take the few objects that offer themselves and ask a whole catalogue of often absurd questions about them. Does it work? How? What made it and of what? And, in parallel, when and where did I last see something like it and what else does it remind me of? And if we are dissatisfied at the time, we repeat the series in the optative mood, making each imperfection in what we have to hand evoke a wish or an ideal. So we set in train a wonderful flow of combinations and associations in our minds, the length and complexity of which soon obscure its humble starting-point.

The objects in my cell were few and bare; I have enumerated them all in the last chapter, except the *gamelle*, or mess-tin, and spoon with which we ate our soup. There was neither comfort nor company in any of them, but they served a brief term of slavery to the orgy of speculation to which confinement drove me. My bed, for example, could be measured and roughly classified with school beds or army beds, according to appearance and excepting the peculiarity of its being hinged to the wall. Yet it was a bed with a pronounced difference from any other. The broad lattice-work of iron laths, which took the place of springs, was unique and almost supernatural in its torment. If I lay on my back, at least one vertebra was wedged in a sharp corner; if I lay on my side, a hip or shoulder-blade or elbow found itself pressed against an edge; and if I lay on my stomach, my nostrils were filled with straw-dust. Yet this bed retained a quality of bed-ness which summoned all my associations with all the beds I had ever known. In it my fears, joys, sorrows and relief were those of bed, not to be found in haystacks or ditches or on the floor, but common to every bed from canopy to canvas.

When I had done with the bed, which was too simple to intrigue me long, I felt the blankets, estimated their warmth, examined the precise mechanics of the window, the discomfort of the toilet (perversely, for its very presence was an unexpected luxury), computed the length and breadth, the orientation and elevation of the cell.

There was also some decoration to be seen, for my predecessors had evidently been better equipped than I. There were smears of oil paint on the walls and a great deal of pencil work, ranging from signatures and salutations to lewd sketches derived from interrupted love-lives. Some had also counted the days, but the longest line of pencil marks was fifty-six, so either their patience or their imprisonment had been short. The first case would have been natural and the second desirable, for if the physical nature of this cell was only to be described by understatement, its spirit or atmosphere defied all words.

The adjectives which sprang to mind were those which might properly be used of stagnant pools, although the place was dry and not obscure; there was an obscenity in this calculated degradation of a human dwelling-place which chilled the heart as no fungoid squalor could. There was no filth, generally no vermin: only the diabolic essence of perversion and the smugly spruce technology of a stock-yard.

Wishfulness came easily after I had taken the measure of this poor furniture. As evening fell the patch of sky over the window changed to pink and violet and red, and its beauty came as a harsh reminder that the world still offered all its favours, as cheaply and lavishly, to all who had not lost their foothold on it.

I was mostly concerned at that time with its abundant food, and calculated that somewhere on the line between me and the setting sun was the restaurant where I had dined last night. If I was to the south, then I would need to cross the dome of the Champs Elysées, if farther east, I could skirt it by the river. I started to water badly at the mouth when I remembered the details of the meal, which was the last I had eaten, and found it hard to think of other things than omelettes, Beaujolais and Brie. And I felt sad at the thought of the comfortable feeling of contentment at the end, and incontinently angry when I considered where I should have been this day, on the banks of the Loire or perhaps already over it. We are adaptable creatures, and flatter ourselves with the conceit that by adapting ourselves to events we master them; therefore it is the irrevocable which causes our greatest humiliation.

I lay awake for a long time that night, pricked into consciousness and fury by the banderillas of might-have-beens and hunger.
And when I woke again in the morning, they returned in a sudden
solid onrush as I looked round me at the walls of concrete and
remembered what had happened yesterday. It was then, too, that
the more remote parts of my life started to parade before me, each
marked with its little label, on which was written, 'I am past and
cannot return'. Whereas yesterday I had cursed an interruption
to the current chapter of my life, now I found myself obliged
to say good-bye to everything that had gone before. Fate, as it
were, had tired of the plot which it had woven round me, of the
people and places past which it had led me, and had torn up the
script, undone the world it had created, and was now wondering
whether or not to do the same to me. From this farther side, the
world that was gone presented a new and unfamiliar face. What
my eyes had once looked upon as things or scenes in themselves
complete and independent of me, my memory saw as unfinished
sketches on a single canvas, drawn higgledy-piggledy in the mood
of each minute, then abandoned, and needing more generous
and skilful artistry than I had given them and an eye of a wider
view than mine to bring them together in harmony and endow
each and all with beauty and meaning.

People, to whom I had given such fickle attention as the casual
mood inspired, looked, as they withdrew from my world to another,
sad and neglected; they had come laden with gifts, but time had
been too short and my interest too mobile, and they were returning with their offerings scarcely touched, weighing on their hearts.
And it was too late to do even the slightest thing. The canvas of life
would never be more than a childish daubing, and the people, if
they remembered, would always be heavy with what they could not
give. I did not know how it would have been otherwise, but I knew
that the record was written and closed and that it made sad reading,
less because it was unpleasant, for most records have their lurid

36

chapters and their tragic incidents, than because it was unfinished. I felt, indeed, rather like a student who is given an hour in which to write an essay, and who, when the time is over and only a phrase written, suddenly knows all the brilliant things he might have said and burns with resentment at their suppression by a silly rule of time.

Of the following days I remember little in particular, because nothing happened, and days in prison are distinguishable only by such rare incidents as from time to time make one of them memorable among its fellows. Although I never lost count of the day of the week or of the date, I followed them subconsciously, and life was divided into longer periods, limited by a state of mind or a physical condition; and it was these more personal symbols than sun or moon which marked out the calendar of this period.

But I became an anchorite with almost the ease of inborn talent, as puppies learn to swim, and in the earliest days I had already established the routine by which I was to live, with little variation, for five hundred and twenty-six days.

Throughout the summer, while it was fine and warm, I slept bare between my two blankets, and when in the early morning I heard the trolley rattling round the floor with the 'coffee' (a euphemism, but it will serve), I put on my trousers and washed under the cold tap. This was an operation which required some skill, for the tap was of the push-button kind and had to be pressed with one hand while the water was scooped up with the other. And when I had done that, my active day was ended. As Economic Man my small doings were quite passive, and as *homo artifex* I was incapacitated by lack of the wherewithal to draw, write or make anything; nor could I even be a student, however poor, since I had nothing to read. The fourteen or more hours of daylight could be filled only by the aimless movement of my body in the cell or by the meandering of thoughts within my head.

Patience is a matter of anticipation. One does not suffer the passing of empty time, but rather the slowness of the expected event which is to end it; the patient mind is fixed on a future happening, not on present inactivity. Nobody can say sensibly to himself, 'I am going to sit still for fourteen hours', and no more, because before the sentence can mean anything to him the hours have to be given substance. But he can look at his watch at ten o'clock, say his sentence and wait quietly until the hands pass twelve o'clock for the second time; or he can recollect some experience of similar or related duration and relive it mentally. It is not, perhaps, strictly true to say that time is only intelligible to the human mind in terms of successive events, but it becomes a statement of practical validity and of mortal clarity in a life where there is little else but time and where events are either undistinguished or so rare that they defy anticipation. For living is largely the experience of succession and becomes rarefied in step with it.

I discovered a sort of clock. On a sunny day I could just see through the frosted glass of my window that while the main part of the wall opposite was of a light colour, a shadow was cast by the gable at the top of it, and this shadow lengthened slightly as the sun rose higher. After the zenith there was a period when I had no sign at all, but late in the afternoon the sun sent one tiny beam on to the wall of my cell above the skylight, and this again cast a shadow which crept upwards for an hour or so and then dissolved. But although this clock was of some help, it was a fickle friend.

Watching it move so slowly was apt rather to snap patience than to smooth it, and in the long run it was best as an occasional encouragement, as when, after a long and tedious afternoon, the sun would suddenly come out and show me that I was further through than I had thought.

There was also a daily event of great importance, at midday, when the soup was served. It was brought round in tubs on the trolley, making a great clatter, and was preceded by a guard who opened a little hatch in the middle of each door. When we heard the noise begin, we stood by the door with our *gamelle* on the shelf inside the hatch. There, for a moment, we could see the outside world, but only in a flash until another guard seized the *gamelle*, half-filled it from a ladle and banged it back on the shelf, slamming the hatch before he moved on to the next cell.

Either before or after the soup was issued, the trolley came round again with the bread ration, about 300 grammes, with a minute piece of fat and sometimes a slice of liver sausage—the small-bore kind—or a small piece of cheese. At first, the soup was never more than cabbage and water, but in 1943 it became thicker and was varied on some days, and there was a daily slice of sausage or cheese. But it never kept us more than barely alive. Later, too, they barred all the hatchways so that the door had to be opened for service, letting us glimpse a little more than a dull Teutonic face: we could see their legs, too, symbols of freedom.

There were thus two halves of the day, and I was never sure which was the harder to endure. The morning was hungry at the outset, but it had a clear and useful end; the evening came in on a relieved stomach, if not on a full one, but its end was hazy and therefore more remote. Sleep was the only end, but sleeping depended upon eating (and sanity depended upon both); and the only thing I could eat at that time was my bread, which I could otherwise use either to shorten the morning wait or to make a whole meal with the soup.

To keep my bread untouched was always difficult, and the more so as time went on and I became chronically hungrier, but I decided early that it was the best course. For there were ten hours in the night during which nothing could happen, nothing be done except lie in bed, and to pass them awake and on an empty stomach was an ordeal which was best avoided. I found it childish, and a matter for disrespect, that I needed so much self-control to keep that small hunk of bread. I felt that a stronger character would have managed so small a task without fuss or frenzy, while for me it was like a stone of Sisyphus, again and again rolling back on me when I thought it would trouble me no more.

But I kept my determination and fought an unceasing war about it, and although I had never troubled to inflict upon myself a discipline which I took irksomely from others, the strange confusion of our language, which brings expediency and moral dignity so close together, made me self-satisfied when I won and ashamed when I was beaten.

To shorten the morning lap of this daily marathon, after I had washed, I used a series of pastimes which I regarded as ridiculous but useful. I started by manicuring myself with a sliver of wood which I managed to peel from the stool. I had never done such a thing before, at least with any but the most perfunctory attention, but now I made a great show of it, partly because the more care I took with it the longer it would last, and partly because I had sentimental memories of being chided for my ill-kept hands and thought that the least I could do now was to make myself as presentable as might be.

But this was all that I could do for my toilet except on one day a week, when the guards brought shaving things round from cell to cell. The soap was bad, the brushes thin and the blades, by the time they reached me, so blunt that they pulled more bristles than they cut. Shaving was supposed to be strictly supervised by the guards, but often they were careless, having more than one prisoner to watch, and at these times I managed to cut my nails too. I had many scruples about this, thinking guiltily of my neighbour's beard, but I am afraid I overcame them and hoped that I would be forgiven. I hated to bite my nails. Yet I never thought to cut a vein.

When the manicure was finished, I sat on my stool and, with what even then appeared ridiculous solemnity, forbade myself to rise again before I had catalogued the counties of England, Scotland, Wales and Ireland and after them the States of America and their capitals, as far as I could remember them. And if after that I still felt that I could sit on for a while, I invented other exercises, such as journeys from one place to another, naming the towns and peoples on the way and listing their languages and trades.

Once, when I was well trained in these austere ways, I managed to sit for a whole morning occupied with questions of geography, and I was pleased with myself for passing the time so diligently. I believed that I was not only conserving energy by sitting still but also that I was keeping my brain in working order by saving it from the sloth of dreaming which it more naturally sought.

When I could sit no longer, I did physical exercises, remembering a warning that one could never tell, even in prison, when fitness would be critical. But I performed them with a vigour much greater than the hope of escape which chiefly justified them, and there is doubt in my mind whether they did more good than harm.

The whole of this programme, which required great concentration and not a little insanity of a self-conscious kind, can normally have lasted little more than an hour. Rarely had the shadow on the opposite wall begun to show when I reached the end of my repertoire and was reduced to the chief stock-in-trade of all those in solitary confinement: pacing up and down the cell.

My abode was some ten feet long by five feet wide. Most of its width was filled by the bed on one side and the table on the other, though they could be lifted on their hinges and laid flat against the wall. I did this during the first day or two and tried walking in a circle, feeling that it would give me a greater sense of liberty, but the experiment proved that the most satisfactory method was to go straight up and down, taking five paces from end to end and pivoting round on the last in such a way as to keep the rhythm even. It was strangely calming and absorbing. Often I would count the rounds, starting sometimes from the window and sometimes from the door; but I generally forgot from which end I had started and so had to make another turn to ensure that I had given full measure—a process which could be interminable.

Sometimes I tried to reckon the time I had passed or the distance I had covered, counting an arbitrary three hundred and sixty rounds to the hour or a speed of one mile an hour. But this was a precarious calculation, since if I started to count too early in the day I would reach the formidable and wearying total of seven hundred and twenty, only to realize that I had completed less than half the course, and this might be the moment when I would think that I could not go on. For the most part, however, I paced up and down unconsciously; the motion and the sound became hypnotic, like the drip of water or the pulse of a drum.

Sometimes a sudden weakness forced me to sit down; sometimes, after the summer, the cold drove me into bed. Then, if I was lucky, I might have been given a new supply of paper—for a purpose quite unconnected with literature—and if I had not already learned its contents by heart, I could read it through and through until I had. Generally, we were given torn and ancient sheets of the *Pariser Zeitung*, but sometimes there were pages of books. Whatever came was interesting.

But if I either had no paper or had drawn the last drop of interest from what remained, I found myself faced with one of those situations which are the embodiment of nonsense, where some rescue from insanity is necessary but none forthcoming, and where madness yet does not leap into the breach. No doubt I would have gone mad, because it takes a well-nourished brain to cope with such an absolute as Nothing, but I regret to say that I threw out the rules of the game on most of these occasions and filled in the nothingness which menaced me by eating my bread. This broke the spell and calmed the animal gnawing at my solar plexus, but it also brought leisurely repentance and anger at my weakness and a hungry night.

Hunger was always in the background. As soon as I had fallen into a steady rhythm of pacing I would drift into daydreams, mixtures of memory and desire, the past retouched to show it as the ideal life for any future. The scenes and episodes varied with the seasons; twenty summers would return in August, twenty springs in April; but at the end of everything there was a meal. I would spend an hour walking in the hills, but it was not the intrinsic pleasure that was most sharp, the freedom and the space, the gradual exaltation of a long ascent, the sudden elation of walking on the level crest, the happy dropping down. These things were fine and beautiful in their way, but they were seen dimly in the background, for the journey's end was its chief delight, and my imagined steps were guiding me surely to supper, with pies and porridge and all the other things that fill you to a stupor.

I even found unfamiliar pleasures in my schooldays, occasions marked by quantities of chocolate; and the drab life of barracks shone with a new brilliance when I remembered its cloying quantities of food. The cheapest stew was reborn as good as a stuffed goose; dry bread was something holy.

Yet for all its persistence, hunger was probably better than food. The lions we put in cages are thought to be well treated if they are well fed, but eating and sleeping are only a small part of even the most bestial existence, only two of the vast pattern of actions which is the life itself, the concert of myriad sights and sounds with their appropriate meanings and reactions, the rituals of courtship and hunting, the customs of the natural community. Hunger lowers the whole vitality, so that after a while these other things are missed less sorely. Thought grows more abstract, sex goes to sleep, and a sort of balance with the empty environment is attained, with only a single giant appetite to disturb it. All the pressures and strainings of the body are, as it were, collected together in the stomach, where they are more safely, if no less painfully, controllable.

I took the soup slowly, drinking the water first and eating the questionable solid afterwards, pretending in this way that it was a meal of two courses. And when it was gone I sat or lay on my bed for a while, because my frivolous memory reminded me that my sister had always insisted that her puppy keep quiet after his meals to get the best out of them, and I thought that what was good for puppies might as well be good for me. But impatience soon made me start walking again on the second lap, which, as I reminded myself in my more pessimistic moods, was seven hours, or two thousand five hundred and twenty rounds, or seven miles.

The first two hours were generally the most difficult, for the soup was a mere *amuse-gueule*, tickling the appetite and tempting me with the suggestion that if I were only to eat my bread as well I could feel comfortably full.

Sometimes I had to resort to the most absurd self-trickery to avoid doing so. I hid the crust under a blanket, or even under the bed, and tried to convince myself that it was not really there. But this was apt to be dangerous: oneself is a treacherous antagonist at bluff; and more than once I found that I was not only eating the forbidden fruit but had convinced myself that it was the wise and proper thing to do.

It was safer to find some line of thought or daydream which I could follow through the first half of the afternoon, until the finger of sunlight on my wall told me that the end was near. Then, as a rule, and unless I was too interested in my own thoughts, I embarked on a musical programme to conclude the day. Being no singer, even to my own taste, I whistled every tune I could remember, the martial ones to make me triumphant over my enemies, the homely ones which made me think of food, and the emotional ones which occasionally, and to my own amusement, brought a conventional tear out of its duct. This was a long programme, which grew as my memory became sharper, and it brought me easily to a point where I could say, 'Now it doesn't matter if I do eat my bread'. And, having reached this point, I found it easy to go on almost forever, at least until what I assumed to be seven o'clock.

It so happened that all forms of music were forbidden, and once or twice my performances were interrupted by the entry of an infuriated sentry.

Our regular guards never worried over such details, but the mean substitutes who replaced them at weekends could only use petty excuses to intrude upon us. The former were for the most part harmless souls, if gruff. The sergeant in charge of the floor was a big blond man, well in his forties, with a bulbous and brutalized nose and hairy brows over eyes which were blue and rather pleasing. Rumours which I heard later had it that he was the brother of the Bishop of Cologne, or some such personage, and he showed consideration for his charges. With me he was silent, so I assumed him to be surly, but he was a guardian angel compared with the Toad and Bat-ears, under whom I suffered later, and on Christmas Day, 1943, when he was on duty for the whole prison, he came into all the cells and asked if the prisoners wanted to attend Mass. I remember that he wished me a happy Christmas.

He had a corporal under him named August. August was small and most easily associable with a plough, or perhaps a pig-sty. His speech was habitually rough, but I suspect that this was a manner which he found expedient rather than desirable.

Lastly, there was a lance-corporal, of whom I can remember little save that he sometimes brought the lavatory paper. I liked none of them at the time, although later contrast made me almost love them, but at least they let me play myself in to supper undisturbed.

I made an even more elaborate ceremony of supper than of soup. In summer I waited for it until the sun was behind the other building and no longer shone into my cell; later in the year, till sunset, judging the moment by the colour of the clouds in the tiny patch of sky which I could see; and finally, when winter came on, till dark, scrupulously estimating the fine degrees of twilight and even reckoning with the moon and the brightness of the stars to make sure that I was not too early. In midwinter I waited even longer, to abbreviate the night, and sometimes a sentry would switch on the light (which was controlled from the passage and only used for spying) and order me to bed. Perhaps he thought that I was hatching an escape. He would have misjudged me gravely, for this moment was the height of my domestication.

When I had finally decided that the time had come, I tried to muster all my capacity for enjoyment in preparation for the feast. But Pascal was right about pleasure. I had looked forward for so long and taken such pains to wait that at least two-thirds of my delight in eating were consumed already in the anticipation.

In summer I ate rather primly at the table, trying to behave as nearly as possible to an ordinary person in the hope that my meal might thus more closely resemble ordinary meals. But in winter I took my food to bed and added to its consolation that of privacy, of that perfect secrecy from the world outside which only a blanket, pulled well over the head, can procure.

Then, for a short while, I could congratulate myself and put away the thought of hunger. But sometimes I tried to do more and told my imagination that it could feast freely on its dreams of loaded tables, stuffed pies and steaming pots, that it could, in a manner of speaking, make hay while the sun shone and reward itself for a day's restraint. But when I tried to gloat in this way I found it tasteless. It was better to profit honestly from what I really had than to make more of it.

As it grew dark a new activity stirred around the prison. In the daytime there was a constant monotone of sergeants and guards shouting to one another; on weekends they went to Paris, leaving the sentries, silent and treacherous in grass-soled shoes, alone with the prisoners in a hush that seemed loud with anxious thoughts. But dusk was the signal for a sudden awakening, like dawn in a garden full of birds. First one voice, then another, and finally a whole chorus started to chatter and shout. Most of them seemed to belong to the building opposite, whose shadow I could dimly see, but a few sounded much closer, above me or below. Only a little of the noise was intelligible, and most of what came to me coherently was names and isolated words.

There would be a cautious *'Allô! Dédé!'*

And then, still quietly: *'C'est toi, Pierrot?* What have you heard?'

'Have you had a parcel?'

This would eventually mount into a complicated conversation, joined by other voices and growing more and more raucous, as if the '*Other spirits attending on Prospero*' had revolted and taken over the script of *Tempest*. There would be action of some kind, too, for I would hear a warning, '*Michel! T'es prêt?*' and then a hushed, or sometimes a confident, '*Vas-y!*' Meanwhile, over the simian babbling, a particularly luscious tenor was wailing a serenade or a loud baritone announcing that '*J'emmerde les gendarmes*'. It was only after I had reached Buchenwald eighteen months later that I learned that the prisoners in the other building were in those days common-law criminals, with nothing respectably resistant about them, but I admired their spirits and envied their adaptability. Even when I was annoyed because their din was violating my carefully won peace there was something sane and soothing about being able to feel common human anger. But I had no desire to take part with them, nor to talk to anyone, unless it had been to order dinner. I wished for company, because that would assure me of material security, but it must be familiar. I wanted nothing of strangers.

Later that evening, the man in the cell next to mine started to tap on the wall. When I understood that he was signalling to me I wanted him to stop, but because I could not make him do so I learned his system and listened to what he said. He had an infantile code, using one tap for A and twenty-six for Z, and it took a great deal of patience to listen to 'w h a t i s y o u r n a m e'. He asked all the obvious questions and some leading ones, and I gave him laconic and untruthful answers. I was suspicious of him and he bored me; the only thing of interest that I learned being that the prison we were in was Fresnes. But he continued in spite of my coolness. I had no wish to hurt him if he was in earnest, but I was selfish and prized my silence, especially the silence of night. For the night, to those who have used it for privacy and sleep rather than as a trysting-place for ghosts and demons, is by instinct and experience a peaceful time, when your surroundings disappear and you may go where you will, and even the deadliest fear is tamed and may be touched and played with.

‖

Chapter 3

For three weeks the Germans made no move in my direction but left me to consider my plight. Nevertheless, I expected them daily, and each time I heard boots outside my door I waited tensely and dismally to be summoned to the next interrogation, dismally because I could not imagine otherwise than that my bluff would be called and my story brought to a swift conclusion. The worst time was in the early morning, because there seemed to be some sort of parading at this time, as if the day's crop of victims was being gathered, and I felt that the hour was dangerous, since my stomach was empty and my mind still smooth and lazy from sleep. But it was almost worse to suppose, as I did alternatively when this hour was past, that there was no routine, and that at any moment all my wit and power of resistance must be available.

After the first few days I gave up all hope that my false identity would have survived. For a little I entertained the kind of romantic hopes that are really despair disguised, toying with the fancy that the French police in Sancerre would see why they were being asked about me and would take my side, or that our own people had managed to alter the archives of the town so as to include my birth there. And I supposed that time waited was time gained, and who could tell that there would not be an invasion or a rising by the French before the autumn? But such figments were an emotional routine, a cushion of never-never keeping the two poles of fear and reality apart. My more honest self knew that a new crisis had to be faced.

The peril was both physical and moral. I was deeply afraid of torture (I cannot imagine that anyone would not be) and I was appalled by the thought of the treachery to which it might reduce me. In England, they had told us that if we were caught we could assume that all we knew would be disclosed, and they had offered us pills to kill ourselves with. I had believed them most readily, but impersonally, not willing to consider my own case as a possibility, and a natural disgust with suicide had made me refuse the precaution; and even now I gave at most only a passing glance at the road which many took as the most honourable and which, in my inner ineffectual heart, I thought the bravest. But at this close range I knew that torture would make me talk, and the extent of my information shocked me. For having been briefed for three missions before finally leaving London, and having moreover been fairly carefully trained, I knew enough about the mechanism of our organization to be a considerable danger to it, especially in these days before large numbers of us were in the field. But although common honour demanded silence on these subjects, some stronger bond required that my three friends in France should be defended. All of them—Madame Terrien, Sébastien and Jacques—had taken me without question at my own valuation, had helped me for the asking, and would be deeply involved if their names were so much as mentioned. And yet it seemed impossible that I should shelter them if the Germans did to me the things that I was imagining. There were a few who resisted the worst punishment and said nothing. There was one young Frenchman who was returned to his mother's house without eyes, teeth, tongue or feature, because he was useless. He had not talked and never would talk again. But they were few and I was not of their number.

I did not believe I had been followed, because I had taken studious measures to prevent it and had doubled them before going to a meeting. It was therefore unlikely that any of my friends were already suspect. But I remembered, and hardly dared to remember, the letter that I had written to Madame Terrien the night before my arrest. There was proof that I knew someone, even though the names and addresses were safely meaningless, and surely, if the Germans had found the letter, as they must, they would merely have to persist in order to find its real destination. The problem was too awesome to be faced reasonably.

However, our disabilities are mercifully balanced, and as the blind are keen of ear, so the faint-hearted may find a ready brain in his head: 'Danger deviseth shifts; wit waits on fear'. My wits in the daytime were as those of a driven hen, but at night they came to roost. Then the bread I had eaten made a yeasty bubbling in my stomach, as comforting as if a hot-water bottle were being turned over and over inside me. Anywhere else, this might have been called indigestion, but in Fresnes it signified the presence of matter in the digestive organs, and this was one of the beatitudes. It compelled stillness and, banishing the anxieties of the body for a while, quieted those of the mind. It was a moment of temporary withdrawal, and while it lasted I found myself inspired by far-fetched and almost absurd ideas of stories I might tell.

I did not give them much credit the next day, when the tramping boots came back to duty and kept me face to face with more realistic images, but I remembered them nevertheless, and when the time came for me to talk I found myself almost unconsciously reciting an anthology of these plots and counter-plots which had

51

been cooked in the post-prandial simmering of an overheated imagination.

Footsteps were always coming to my door. They passed, but not before they had asked the eternal questions. Did they handcuff you? Did they explain what would happen? Would it be short or long? And before they finished their business, did they grant you a last wish, and what would you ask? I wanted to ask for an escort to take me to the Crémaillère for an eight-course dinner, but felt this to be slightly improper. A last letter seemed more decorous, but what good would it do even if there were some relief in writing it? Perhaps the best course was to ignore the offer frigidly, although it seemed a pity not to mark such a definite departure in some fitting way. We have an instinct for celebration.

It seemed important only that I should be able to keep my knees straight at the critical moment, and from this point of view a good meal would be desirable. I told myself that courage was more necessary, but the notion had a meaningless ring to it. Courage serves in face of pain or hardship, but one cannot face death. Death is a word which presents no real target to the mind's eye.

Imagine a bare plot of ground with a wall around it; see yourself standing against the wall, with soldiers in front of you, aiming their rifles at you. Imagine the flashes and the sudden start, and the pain of bullets ploughing through you. Only so far can you imagine. Death has retreated like the rainbow's end. And if you go further with the scene, and see the body lying crumpled before the wall and other soldiers coming to remove it on a barrow, you are using a playwright's licence. For this body is not yours, but another: unable to imagine the feelings of your own self after dying, you have skilfully substituted an impersonal dummy for your body.

At first, you were the actor, the passive victim of your own subjective sensibilities; but now you have slipped into the stalls and are watching actions in which you have no part and of which you know nothing subjectively. You can imagine the simple physical perishing of someone else, but you can only track your own death to the threshold of its lair, where it lies hidden from you.

For death, as a word, is a limitless negation. It means life with a minus sign *ad infinitum* and is therefore irrational. But because we see it happen to other people, or see what we take for the evidence that it happens to them, we do not bother with the infinitude but concentrate upon rationalizing the negative.

I said to myself: 'If I have one apple and two baskets and take the apple out of one basket and put it in the other, I can describe the first as "basket minus apple" and know all about it, but I cannot make sense of the apple with that word *minus* before it until I have said "other basket plus apple". Then I understand everything.' And it was clear to me that we perform much the same logical trick with life.

Having an immediate personal interest in the problem, I performed two tricks. First, I tried to deceive the problem itself by saying that by life I understood all the pleasant things that used to happen to me and that dying would mean simply transferring these things into another dimension. But this only meant that I was sad at the thought of leaving all the joys of life and wished them back. It did not really mean that I had invented a heaven for myself. And the second trick I performed was the same manipulation by which mankind in all his forms and ages has tried to provide an ending for his story. I postulated a life 'hereafter', quite different from the 'life here'.

This process of imaginative compensation is as natural as eating. We have a vacuum, a perfect secret, proposed to us as our end and we immediately set about filling it up and revealing it. But I would say here that I was never seriously convinced by my own attempts to do so as long as I regarded death as a thing which might happen tomorrow or in ten minutes. Indeed, the only form in which I could clothe my speculations was the stereotyped Heaven-and-Hell which we were taught from earliest childhood, and this seemed to me much less satisfactory as a metaphysical doctrine of survival than as the carrot-and-stick to reinforce an ethical persuasion. And I was beyond the reach of either stick or carrot, or at least beyond their benefits.

Nevertheless, there is something compelling about Hell. Heaven is a vague and rococo notion; it cannot be held very firmly in the mind, which is only baffled by memories of haloes and cherubim. But as for Hell, we are shrewd folk and more apt to look the gift horse in the mouth than the kicker in the heel: the faintest hint of suffering has our immediate respect. Consuming fires and parching thirst convey a picture which our simple minds can grasp.

Moreover, the system which places Hell at the end of the chain leads us to it by way of our breaches of its moral rules. As I remember it, the morality on which I was raised was really no more than prudence. If you do certain things, it said, you will go to Hell; if you do not do them you will go to Heaven, which is much too difficult a place to be explained. This is a negative doctrine. It depicts in clear and practical terms the place not to go to, the reason—specially vivid—for not going there, and the things not to do in order to avoid it. It does not bother to recommend a positive way to a desirable end, and the hazy promises it makes are considered good enough for a person busy with self-protection from eternal fire. The result is that when we come to a time of reckoning, and especially when we contemplate death, we are more apt to retrace our deviations than the distance we have travelled. And then, though I speak for myself alone, it is not easy to imagine a hereafter that is not hellish.

Limited as I was by the particular traditions among which I had lived, I found it difficult to see the way out of this logic. But I was not convinced by it, partly because it was almost too logical and partly because it left out of consideration all the greater part of life which was quite outside the scope of moral rules and prohibitions. I repented many sins of omission and commission, but I regretted at least as much the loss of the things I loved. Why should a lot of miserable 'sins' have such paramount importance in what was the transference of a whole life? Sins are mostly the work of the body, which dies, but it is the soul which is not allowed to die but is kept in eternal torment for the shortcomings of its carcase. Yet, if there is a soul, it is surely there that happiness is—or was—enjoyed.

Such thoughts as these flitted uneasily through the light atmosphere of my head, like fledgelings called too early to a long migration. But at so short a distance from the nineteenth century and given the proper churching of an English schoolboy for some dozen years, anyone may expect to find thoughts of eternity, and especially of eternal Hell, colouring the prospect of an early death. But he will also hope, and in particular will base his hope on the idea, planted by the same tradition, that the individual is bonded only to God, and that God deals with him with mercy and justice, making the law to suit the accused rather than the punishment to fit the crime. Perhaps he will have forgotten the reasons for which he was taught to hope, but he will hope none the less.

Early in my imprisonment—I suppose it was the second Sunday, since my memory always worked strictly to the calendar—I found myself in a daydream walking back from the old church in Herefordshire where we used to be taken every Sunday in the holidays. The fields had their August warmth and yellowness, the hop-yards stood like orderly jungles waiting for the pickers, there were blackberries in the hedges and thirsty bullocks resting in their shade. And across the stile and through the gate there was lunch.

Like most of my contemporaries I regarded going to church as work on the day of rest. I paid no particular attention to what was said there, for it seemed more manly to concentrate upon a strict indifference to spiritual things, which savoured of girlishness, to stand stiffly with self-conscious grimness and to sit rather than to kneel. One must be pharisaically scrupulous about putting a penny in the plate and sleep stoically through the sermon. But Sunday lunch was important, and its importance, over all those years, now made my mouth water more than ever.

Nevertheless, instead of rushing forward to gloat over pictures of roast beef and Yorkshire pudding, my memory seemed to fumble back a little way for something which had been said in church.

The vicar was an old and venerable man, with a fault in his speech, and we claimed as children that we could understand nothing of what he said. Now all I could remember were the opening words of his service, which as far as I know he never varied: 'I will arise, and go to my father, and will say unto him, Father, I have sinned against heaven and before thee and am no more worthy to be called thy son.'

My reaction to this piece of recollection was like that of the Mole in *The Wind in the Willows* when he caught a whiff of scent from his old home while walking back to the riverbank with Mr. Rat. It was familiar but not immediately recognized; it was strong, but not as strong as the pleasures that lay ahead. But at a distance it came back again and I remembered where it came from. I also remembered more: 'And he would fain have filled his belly with the husks that the swine did eat and no man gave unto him.' What would I not give for a few husks! I was not too clear as to what they were, but they sounded solid and satisfying.

There were other obvious points in common between me and the Prodigal Son, for I had defied my parents and squandered my money on riotous living in what I supposed to be much the same way. But there was also a great point of difference, for this was one of the parables where the culprit was not destined to be fallen upon by robbers and killed: history, alas, seemed once more bound not to repeat itself. But it was beyond my powers of discipline and resignation to refuse to hope for the exception, and in spite of the evidence of my fate I began to think about the chances of a happier outcome.

Hope and fear changed places in my mind as in a farmer's looking for harvest weather. The sunset was good, but there is a west wind, which should bring rain; the stars are bright, but the weather forecast mentioned a disturbance. The Prodigal Son got a fatted calf, but Ananias died for a pretty common sort of lie. Such is superstition: half-knowledge and wishes put together with anxiety, fear and hope compressed in equal parts.

Eventually, like Mole, I decided that I was near home. It was a poor home, to be sure, not built on reason but on legend, and surrounded not with the formal gardening of the intellect but with the endless hazy pasture land of hope. Knowledge and reason had failed to serve me, saying only of my problem that they could find no answer to it. But I wanted an answer, as everyone must, and the old and often despised parable had given one: that I could hope. I could not be certain (reason could have found certainty, if there was any) but I could hope. Who was I to pull this to pieces with clever dialectic? What tired man looks at the legs of a chair if the cushions are comfortable?

'Bring forth the best robe, and put it on him; and put a ring on his hand, and shoes on his feet; and bring hither the fatted calf, and kill it; and let us eat and be merry.'

These were the words I needed to hear, and I would not imperil them with wit. Here were rest and fullness, and if my stomach were still empty, there was a calf to come. It was assured, and who was I to doubt?

So I slept that night, dreaming of banquets and homecomings.

\|\|\|

Chapter 4

On the morning of the fourth Tuesday a sergeant burst into my cell as I was trying to wash under the tap. The sun was up, but it was early, and the trolley had not yet been round with the 'coffee'; and I felt even more discountenanced than I had expected when he barked at me to put on my shirt and coat and leave with him. I felt small and impotent, a mere thing to be moved, inert but not resistant.

We jib at routines when we most observe them, but unpleasant disturbances make us glorify them, and I felt that there was something mean and dangerous in being fetched away before breakfast. My silly mind, full of fetishes, insisted that the missing ration of dirty water was my only source of strength and, eventually, of salvation. I wanted to suggest, as I fumbled with my coat-sleeves, that we should wait until it came, but all my dry and submissive tongue could manage was to ask weakly where I was going. The reply was given in one word: *Tribunal*.

This laconic answer so surprised me that I came a little way back to my senses. For I had in my confusion taken for granted that I was bound straight for the place of execution. Half a minute earlier I could have told accurately what it is like to walk the last few steps on this earth. Or, more truthfully, someone able to read my mind could have told, for I had lost the power of reason or introspection, and the expressive part of my brain could only toy with conventional inanities, like a parrot's speech. The place, the other actors, primitive representations of humiliation and helplessness, figures of distant ignorant mourners: such things came and went confusedly across the screen of my imagination, like the jerky unreal figures of an old silent film. But I was not myself among them, being somewhere behind the scenes, quietly out of control like a free clockwork.

The word *Tribunal* made an end of that. It brought up a picture of hard-faced, tight-collared German officers, unpleasant indeed, but unconsciously the repositories of hope, because they were not in themselves final but only a stage towards finality. I could also imagine myself among them and could therefore concentrate again on a point of reality. To be sure, the hope to be found was modest, and my wilder dreams were properly put to flight, for the bright part of the cloud is at the fringe, not at the centre, and rescue by insurrection, invasion, doctored archives and the rest could not be thought of with the plain fact of a grisly sergeant a yard in front of me. Romance was gone, but I could touch once more the little disembodied hand of hope.

It was therefore in the fear of a fresh engagement with the police rather than in the fear of death that I was driven to the ground floor. I tried to remember all the astute stories I had planned to tell them, but I was too smitten with panic and could only remember my fears. If the sergeant had asked me a few questions then and there I should probably have told him all I knew.

There was already a row of nine or ten other prisoners on the ground floor when I arrived there feeling like a solitary stray goat before my private shepherd. I looked down the line as I fell in at the end but found no one whom I knew or recognized. They were an undistinguished gathering to look at, and I remember feeling a little disappointed with them. Unkempt and bearded, without collar or tie, their shoes gaping open at the top where the laces were missing, they had moreover a look of indistinction, or perhaps of extinction, which came from the deliberate or accustomed banishment of all expression from their faces. In one there might be a flicker of doubt, in another a spark of jauntiness, but the company as a whole was dour and drab.

It is a curious reflection that a man's face may wear its most ordinary complexion when his heart is fighting its direst and most noble battles (whether winning or losing); but I was glad to be among these people, because they showed me at least that it was not necessary to swagger falsely in distress. Many people still live under the illusion that the great and trying moments of life must be met in mediaeval style, with a conventional nobility of gesture and expression, but the truth is that the style is at least irrelevant, because such moments are of private, not public conflict and, the more deeply they are dwelt in, the less openly are they revealed.

A *feldwebel* read our names from a list, standing stiffly and contriving to inject a mild contempt into his version of our inoffensive syllables. We were turned into file and marched down the long underground tunnel which linked the different buildings of the prison. Untidy riflemen escorted us along the flanks and at each end. We made a dismal scene, not elemental and sombre like a Siberian droving, but decorated with the shabby and factitious respectability of mild little *bourgeois*. The ugly, drab, ill-fitting uniforms and the pretentious, padded suits made it hard to believe that real harshness or real heroism was related to that small procession.

It was only a short walk to the other end of the tunnel, but long enough for me to lose the sense of company which I had begun to feel. I became a stranger again, a foreigner intruding, a player in the wrong colours. The Frenchmen were where they should be, or at least where some of them inevitably must be: they were, so to speak, true, while I was a degree removed from truth: and the awareness of falsity put a moat, or a *cordon sanitaire*, round me so that, if the guards had been suddenly withdrawn, I should have been embarrassed by the conversation of my companions.

Although I passed six times through the entrance of Fresnes, I cannot recall a single detail of its appearance, being undoubtedly always too preoccupied with the anxieties which, paradoxically for a prison, attended upon entry and exit in almost equal number. On this occasion there was little time to look; we were marched straight into a police-van and locked in tiny individual boxes, windowless and so small that every part of the body was buffeted against the walls when we moved over the paving-stones. In spite of the guard's warning to keep silence, the others started talking as soon as we left, making me wonder that strangers who could not even see each other could enter at once into so lively a conversation. I was powerless to take part, struggling against the paralysis of my brain to remember the details of the story I had prepared, but I heard a mention of Dieppe.

My heart gave a little leap at the sound of the name, assuming that it spelled invasion, but I could gather nothing clear from the short comments. There was a halt, probably at the Cherche-Midi prison, and a little later the van pulled up finally and the doors of the boxes were opened one by one as somebody called the names. The last name was mine, and I climbed out into a courtyard which I recognized as the rue des Saussaies.

I was received by the small man of the pair who had arrested me. He took me silently but purposefully in a lift to the upper office in which the first interrogation had taken place, where the big man was waiting. After making me sit down, the two of them went and talked in undertones at the other end of the room. A few minutes later, a woman was brought in and seated by a window opposite me. She started to make signs to me and to mouth questions, but I was wary and only smiled until the big man shouted at her to keep quiet. In a little while someone fetched her away.

As soon as the woman had gone the little man picked up a newspaper and, crossing the room, flung it on my knee, saying:

'Voilà votre invasion!'

The largest and boldest type I have ever seen announced the complete failure of the Canadian landing at Dieppe, which had occurred sometime before. Well-chosen photographs made doubt impossible. Faced with flaming tanks and columns of prisoners, I could not say, as we used to say of disasters in other circumstances, that this was the enemy's only success amid a series of defeats. I believed every word and more, and my belief shattered me; but at all costs I must make no sign of it, so I kept reading.

The little man spoke again after a minute.

'You may well be disappointed,' he said. 'It is a pity you were caught before you could carry out your orders.'

Despair had made me so sensitive that I understood immediately the importance of what he had said so lightly. He was suspecting me, in effect, of complicity in the preparation of the Dieppe landing, and since my orders and the chance that I had complied with them expressly denied me access to the east bank of the Seine, I concluded that he did not know much about me. The reasoning was most imperfect, because for all I knew there had been other landings farther west, but I was so concentrated upon Dieppe, lying there like the end of the world on my knee, that I jumped immediately to this conclusion, which was, I think, not only partly true, but also a most serviceable basis for my future answers. For it gave me above all things confidence that my opponents were acting on very little information, that if they wanted more they must ask me for it, and that, in the broad sense, they could not confirm or refute anything which I told them of which I had not left evidence on my trail.

I looked up at the little man rather vaguely and said:

'I don't understand.'

'It is simply,' he replied, with an air of patient pedagogy, 'that the invasion you were supposed to help has failed, and you are here.'

'All I can see,' I persisted, 'is that there has been a British raid and it seems to have failed. But I don't see where I come into it.'

He shrugged his shoulders and gave me a wicked little look.

'It doesn't matter,' he said. 'We shall soon see.' And he went back to resume his muttering with his crony.

A few minutes later an officer came in dressed in the uniform of a major in the Gestapo. He was dark and wiry, more Latin than German, with a ruthless, wolfish face. The other two stood up abruptly at his entry but greeted him somewhat casually, a blend of the forms of welcome used by the meticulous Prussian and the careless gangster. The newcomer crossed the room and spoke to them, giving no sign that he had noticed me, but after a short while he took a packet of cigarettes from his pocket and, turning and seeming to see me for the first time, offered me one and lit it for me. Then he turned his back on me and continued to talk to the others for perhaps twenty minutes.

As I watched the three of them and tasted delicately my cigarette—of which I felt slightly ashamed since it was the gift of an enemy—I could no longer concentrate on what I should say nor guess at what I should be asked. I was full of foreboding but yet more full of resignation: unable to foresee exactly, I could only wait in fear of disgracing myself but with no great spirit of resistance.

Suddenly the major turned and strode across the room and struck me in the face with a swing of his open hand roaring:

'*Wie heisst Du?*'

I knew now what was to come, but although in my fear that violence would prove too much for me I had foreseen and imagined and exaggerated it, the first impact still took me by surprise. There is a sense of shame following an unanswerable blow which has nothing of fear in it but which is more demoralizing than any pain. I now felt that all my thought and planning was in vain and that I was before something which was irresistibly compelling, almost hypnotic. But I had to answer a question and to do so I had to think, which restored a little of my balance and saved me from utter rout.

Since my arrest I had perceived that on no account during an interrogation must I allow myself to be tortured to a point where I should lose my capacity for clear thought, and now, seeing that however much my nationality might be in question there was little or no exact knowledge of my origins or doings, I understood that if I were to become slow of wit I might make slips which would offer loop-holes for further questions and thus enable them little by little to pry from me details about my connections which were at present secure. So suddenly all the disjointed thoughts which had been streaming through my head during the past three weeks fell into place and bore the outline of a plan.

Sooner or later I must talk, before I was bullied from my senses but after an inquisition long enough to let them think that I had submitted. And I saw how easily I could interweave the fictitious story which I had imagined with the truth which I could not deny. But my adoption of this solution was scarcely conscious, for my senses were filled with the menace of my opponent.

'*Wie heisst Du?*' he roared again, and I looked at him as calmly as I could and replied:

'Blanchard.'

He came in again savagely, hitting and kicking and swelling with fury as I parried or avoided his blows. Then the big man came and held me from behind while the little one put a pair of rigid handcuffs on my wrists. Then the major attacked again, nastily now and without anger. In a pause the little man, who was still the only one to speak French, said:

'There is no use in denying your real identity. We know it already. There is worse than this to follow if you are obstinate.

We have special rooms downstairs.'

And the major roared again:

'*Wie heisst Du?*'

And I again, for it was not yet enough although I was growing dumb with pain and appalled at the temerity which I would have to show to lie again:

'Blanchard. If you know my identity already you know that is my name. Why go on asking?'

The bluff had no effect, and the major resumed his attack. He must have had much practice to have become such an expert, for although every blow told, he avoided with great skill dealing any which would give me the quick release of unconsciousness.

Time was beyond reckoning, but it dragged eventually to a moment where coherent thought was slipping willy-nilly away, and with something of the deliberate but reluctant improvidence with which a parachutist leaves his aircraft I emitted a sound of defeat. For in a strange way it now seemed harder to start my new deception than to brazen out the old and broken one. The major stopped at once, turned on his heel and stalked across the room with the indifference of a Hollywood gunman returning his pistol to his pocket.

The little man spoke again.

'It will be better if you speak now. He is getting impatient. But mind that you tell the truth. If you don't things will be much worse.'

I bowed my head in acquiescence, being ashamed of this posture of cowardice and of the scorn which I knew they were feeling. Also I feared that to start talking meant to go on talking and that in the end, for all my good intentions and beginnings, I would be unable to resist and would allow my mind to spill out uncontrolled like a breached dam.

The major came back from the end of the room and leaned uninterestedly against the desk, and the small man began his interrogation.

'What is your real name?'

I gave it.

'And your first name?'

I gave that too.

He showed a momentary flicker of doubt and looked at the major, who did not appear to understand. Then he asked:

'Are you sure you are telling the truth?'

'Of course,' I replied.

'And what is your profession?'

'I am an Army officer.'

'Quite so. And how do you come to be here?'

His tone was becoming complacent and sardonic as he became surer of offering my head in sacrifice to the high priest at his side. But I had chosen this opening carefully in order to guarantee my credit for what was to follow. If a man were to lie in such circumstances, I reasoned, the two points which I had admitted would, in most people's minds, be those about which he would lie longest. I had admitted my identity, enough in itself to warrant my execution: why, therefore, should I bother to lie about anything else? And if the telling of those two truths at the same time pandered to my real desire to give in altogether, it was well so; our greatest determination is frail and not to be overtaxed, and this little adventitious easement of the strain relaxed and cleared my mind so that, although I was still overawed by the leap I was about to take, I knew what I had to say and felt able to command the rest of the conversation.

'I think,' I said, after a pause, 'that if you don't mind I had better tell this story myself from the beginning. I cannot think very clearly after all this, and you can always ask me questions afterwards.'

There was a short, whispered consultation between the three, after which the little man said to me severely:

'Very well, but remember, we want the truth. We Germans

do not like liars. And go slowly, because what you say must be written down.'

Meanwhile, the big man had put paper into a typewriter and was sitting before it, fingering the keys with his stubby fingers. He was incongruous, this oaf at the machine of letters, but he was a blessing in absurd disguise. For if he was to write the statement it must be translated to him, and therefore the construction of it would be slower and the dove-tailing easier.

'All right,' I said. 'Shall I begin?' And when the little man nodded I went on to give an almost true history of myself with many insertions of references, up to the month of April, 1940. In that month I had in fact gone with my regiment to northern Norway, but here history was remade.

'My uncle,' I told them, 'was at that time commanding a brigade of the Highland Division, and since they were part of the Expeditionary Force in France, I managed to get myself seconded to him as interpreter.'

This lie had merit, for not only is nepotism a fault easily attributed to those whom one despises but the uncle moreover happened to be true, although, as they would find to their inconvenience, he had later died as a prisoner-of-war and could therefore neither confirm nor deny my story. Obviously they would (and in fact did) ask for the names of other officers, but that was not difficult, especially in the Highland Division, and if the officers I named proved reticent about their brigadier's 'interpreter', the Germans would as likely as not ascribe it to their unwillingness to get me into trouble. There were questions, too, about the position of the brigade at that time, but although I knew nothing of it, it did not seem probable that they would verify my answers as long as I gave them realistically.

So the story went on. The German attack came, and the British advance and retreat. Finally, the unbroken division was cut off on the cliffs of St. Valéry-en-Caux.

'You mean St. Valéry-sur-Somme?' interrupted the little man, advertising his trap with the hint of a smile.

'No,' I said. 'St. Valéry-en-Caux. I'll show you the two on the map.' And the protest was waived.

In the end the division had to give up. It could not be taken off by sea and the Germans had locked it on the headland. So the march to Amiens started, as I supposed.

'There was a huge amount of traffic on the road, and many of us saw how easy it would be to slip out of the column. Especially for me, because I could speak French, and once I had changed my clothes I could easily reach the Spanish frontier. So that's what I did. I slipped out of the column about fifteen kilometres before Amiens.'

There was no comment. The little man dispassionately translated to the big one, who banged on his typewriter, and the major eyed me in a calculating way.

The next part of the story was easy, for I had known an officer from another division who had in fact escaped from about the same point, so that all I needed to do was to make myself his companion. And in this way, not unconvincingly, I reached the Pyrenees. Here, however, the real difficulties began, for I must account for two whole years spent in France, and I was at a loss to explain how I, who spoke French well, had failed to make the simple journey which hundreds had managed comfortably on simple Cockney. But they gave me no chance to stop for thought, so I embarked upon the recital of such a series of catastrophes as my real self would never have survived.

'When we arrived near Pau,' I told them, 'an unhealed wound gave my companion so much trouble that we had to rest for a while.' I nearly attributed the wound to myself, until I remembered that I had no suitable scar.

'What was the name of the place, and how did you rest?'

'I forget the name of the place, but it was a farm about ten kilometres on the road to Tarbes.'

'What was the name of the farmer?'

'Ybarnegaray.' The first Basque name that came to my head.

'Go on.'

'We stayed in a barn for a few days and went on.'

'Who fed you? The farmer?'

'Yes, but I don't think he realized quite who we were.'

I hoped there was no farmer of that name who would be victimized on our mythical account; if they found there was none it would make little difference to my story as a whole.

When he nodded to me to continue I told how we had made our way to the frontier and had found a party of smugglers who were willing to take one, but not more, of us across. Whereupon, with quasi-Teutonic but improbable chivalry, I had surrendered the privilege to my companion. (Indeed, I had to be quit of him at some point.) I had wandered back to the farm, but the farmer had been too frightened to keep me longer, so I had drifted about sleeping and eating where I could, until I had fallen sick with a high fever. There followed imprisonment and escape from the French in Marseilles, at a time when there had been so many such incidents that they were not all likely to have been properly recorded, finance from an American newspaperman and concealment in the Camargue.

It was a most improbable tale, and I had some difficulty in dating it conveniently, but it came most naturally to my lips, as if I was being prompted from the wings each time a fatal gap threatened to halt me. It was, moreover, so vague as to be almost impossible for them to check in detail. So I brought myself through until the preceding May, when I supposed myself to have decided in despair to make for the Channel coast and try to find a boat which would take me across to England. I thus accounted, and this part could be verified, for my apparently aimless wandering about Normandy.

And so it ended. There were questions and cross-questions, dates and places were travelled over and over again, but the story once told never left me for a moment, and although I tried not to be too glib I had an answer for everything. Finally, the big man took the last sheet of paper from his machine and handed me a copy of the whole statement as he had written it. I was bidden look at it and sign, but remembering that my German was limited to two or three words, I simply signed.

My three judges appeared a little taken aback.

'I hope that *was* the truth,' said the little man doubtfully. 'Your signature as an officer is your honour, and if you have signed nothing but lies you will find we will refuse you any respect.'

I always think of him as the 'little man'.

The lift took me down again, and after a short wait in the old cell on the courtyard another Black Maria bumped me back to Fresnes. The little corporal of the top floor, August, called to escort me to my cell, stared at me and muttered:

'*Aber du lieber Mann!* That was a Tribunal!'

Perhaps he suffered from vicarious conscience, for he was almost kindly as, staring wide-eyed at my altered features, he led me upstairs and pointed to the *gamelle* of cold soup which had been waiting for me since noon.

'*Essen*', he said; '*gut!*' and went out, locking the door with the two heavy clicks, but, I thought, not quite as roughly as usual.

For a while, however, I left the soup untouched, and the bread beside it. Now that the day was past, the long-awaited summons answered and no damage done, some inflated rubber animal inside me eased, and I felt a great vacuum being sucked downward through my body.

It was nearly dark, and I sat emptily on my bed, beginning to feel my aches. Yesterday I had thought that I had come near to believing in God and that there was some hope in life. Then I looked again at the awful rank-smelling tin of old cabbage soup, comparing it with the fatted calf and remembering, as it were with despair, one who had told me not long ago that 'the New

Testament is the finest known piece of propaganda, because it tells people exactly what they want to hear'.

It was so clear to me now. Men sought an explanation of what they could not understand, comfort when they were desolate and hope when they despaired. So they invented God in their imaginations, a universal providence to feed their wants. The Greeks, who were a curious and thoughtful people, came by their Pantheon to explain the many mysteries of nature; the Jews in their misfortune claimed a Victorian father who accounted for such few amenities as came their way, but even more adequately for their unceasing tribulations. And then, to crown all, came the 'finest piece of propaganda', rivalling all the theologies in explanation and in consolation. But how could it be reconciled with that pan of putrid soup?

With that I stopped thinking, because, after all, there was no further room for thought. I sat until a stealthy footstep outside the door brought back antagonism and made me rise. The shutter of the peep-hole slid up, and the eye behind it found me at my usual exercise; and as it waited long and watched, thinking itself unnoticed, I sat on the stool and started to eat.

||||

Chapter 5

The next morning found me more hopeful than I had ever been. I had slept through the reaction, and now the purely physical aches were as satisfying and relaxing as those of a good day's exercise. My tale was a feeble one, but my inquisitors seemed—at this distance—to have minds not far from feeble, and if they checked it in the way I had intended they would come first, in official lists, to my own authenticated identity, and secondly, in their own lists of prisoners, to that of my uncle. My chances of being taken for a prisoner-of-war would therefore brighten. Then they would probe in the Unoccupied Zone and find a dead trail; but collaboration between the French and German police was by no means cordial, and with fortune on my side they would come back to the last part of the story, investigating the hotels in which I had stayed in the Occupied Zone, where they would again find nothing but the simple truth. And then?... But at this point I abandoned calculation and sailed gaily off to a dreamland of camps of prisoners- of-war, where only English was spoken, where no one worked, and where daily arrived thousands of enormous parcels of food. Into the parcels I delved and romped in a heap of hams and plum puddings and bathed in condensed milk, until at length my rhythmic feet were quite disjointed from my spirit.

For several days I lived in a mad exaltation of confidence, thinking of little but the good days to come. Only a realism most unnatural to me made me interrupt my rapture from time to time to go over the story I had told, see where it would fail and try to devise a sequel for the next interrogation.

I was disturbed from my reverie one day by the sound of the trolley outside. 'Soup', I told myself, not realizing that the morning had passed so quickly and congratulating myself on the fortunate and absorbing theme which had made time so harmless. This was in truth the secret of living in prison, and perhaps of all living: to dream of pleasant things when there were none real to be enjoyed, and to make the most of the few real pleasures. For of pleasures there was at least one, since I had grown used to prison food. Especially in the evening, after I had jealously kept my bread to make my solemn supper, I was learning to enjoy tasting the bran and the corn in it. For my sense of smell and taste had become acute, perhaps because I no longer smoked, so that I could detect the essence of the raw food, which reminded me of bags of uncooked oatmeal and great pails of bran mash given to horses, of an honesty not to be found in ordinary meals.

So I was pleased with myself, almost jubilant, when the trolley rattled to a halt near my door. But the hatch was unlocked roughly, and as I held out my mess-tin a fist met it and banged on to the little shelf the lump of bread, split in two parts, which was the ration for the day. This had happened before, quite often, and it had always annoyed me, because it meant that I must keep the bread uneaten for an hour longer, and an hour in which I was more impatient than at any other time.

Today I raged childishly at the breach of the convenient order.

All had been well, the morning had passed and I was happy. Some diabolic spirit had lured me into complacency and then had poked this jibe at me, as if to say, 'I'm sorry, but you're still in prison'. The bread was a taunt and I sensitive, and in my fury I broke off a crumb and ate it. Even as I did so I knew, with that deep intuition which becomes almost a second self to the unreasonable, that my day was done. Always, or almost always, I had been able to keep my bread if I had kept it whole, but were I to taste the tiniest morsel my empty stomach clamoured and twisted until it had made me satisfy it.

I broke off another small piece and chewed it in a pondering way, trying to make myself realize the enormity of what I was doing, of the unending day and night to be passed without food; but I could not make the future hunger more real than the present, nor could I hold myself in by self-mockery. I decided to compromise by eating only one half of the crust (a compromise which had never succeeded), but the inner voice insisted more loudly that it was too late; and this time I heard it and acquiesced.

Pondering the vanity of the comfort I had believed in earlier, I sat on the bed and slowly ate until there was nothing left. Then the trolley started to clatter with the soup. Only half an hour had stood between me and the empty night. *If only*...nowhere can we escape our conditional mood.

Hunger was a monster of many heads and arms, thinking evilly against my thoughts and striking wickedly at all my weaknesses. Loneliness, weakness, the binding walls, memory, desire—it took them all into its service, drawing my guard to one, then striking at the other, letting me slink into the stronghold of a daydream, then pulling me painfully out. Time healed each scar, but time was endless, so that the wounds were continually renewed; and the knowledge that this was so was itself another weapon against me. Patience was always at its limit, but the limit was always advanced. By the end of the day I was chastened and sought neither to hope nor to regret. I had neither will nor dream, only a vague interrogation of mood, passive and general, querying, even querulous, but not curious in particular.

The next two days passed in the same mental doldrums. I made no effort to keep my bread until the evening but ate it promptly as it came, trying to appreciate the fleeting midday fullness. But when I woke on the Saturday morning and remembered the long depressing silence of the weekend to come, when the bread was issued early on both days, I cursed myself for having let my control slip so far that I could no longer regain it. But I cursed weakly, with no thought of remedy.

Resistance, however, is as spontaneous as the drawing of breath, and before an hour was past I had determined that I would try again. I cast about for new stratagems to conquer time, new hiding places where I could pretend to forget my bread, and soon exhausted myself by fighting the battle before the enemy's approach. And, seeing defeat arranged in spite (as I thought) of my good intentions, I sought a scapegoat, and at once there came back the seeming mockery of that 'finest piece of propaganda'. Fine it was indeed: *'ask and ye shall receive.... What man of you, if his son ask him bread, will he give him a stone...?'* It was easy to sit and listen to the kindly, hopeful words so long as the Sunday beef was sizzling in the oven and there was no need to ask. This was the testing time and the words had proved barren.

A remote but persistent memory of scholarship pulled me up. 'Loose criticism,' it said, 'is both unwise and unjust. To judge sentences you must weigh each word and not simply ascribe a meaning to the full stop. What about "Father" and "son" and "ask"? Did you consider yourself as a son and ask for anything?'

This was a somewhat embarrassing thought to me, but in the end I had to admit my unfairness. I had not considered the proposition so and indeed doubted whether I could. But was there not another passage which said that God knew what you needed before you did yourself? Still, the argument held, because at least the relationship was inherent, and I wondered awkwardly whether it was possible at this late stage to ask God for help. There was certainly no other possible source, though it seemed that the 'worth trying' frame of mind would be unlikely to produce results. I believed conversationally in God as I believed in molecules: as I could credit the likelihood of microscopic physical division without seeing it, so I could also admit that there must logically be a Beginning or a First Principle. Such a Beginning was as likely to be an impersonal as a personal one, for I had not bothered to inquire into the meaning of such philosophy as I had been taught.

I had been apt to consider, as the shallow science of our age had urged, that for practical purposes the world was a finite object for the analysis of Man, who was also finite but on a superior plane from which he could master the world with an all-powerful tyranny of algebra. I was not so critical as to ask what the achieved mastery was worth or how well men's needs were satisfied by its progress, for I was most cogently self-centred, and if I inquired, it was after my own profit from the arrangement and not after that of mankind. At this moment in particular the inquiry was limited to: 'Am I helpless or not, and if not, how is help going to come?'

The word 'prayer' scarcely occurred to me. Perhaps the unnaturalness of its old associations forbade its formulation. 'To ask' was the operative verb; but to ask whom? A Beginning was too bleak, the relationship too distant, and it was only by an unsatisfactory process of imagination that I could endow it with the quality of mercy. It was the old trap of anthropomorphism, but what of it? There are no doubt as many views of God as there are creatures.

When the bread was brought round it was the same meagre ration as on other days, and immediately I felt an impulse to seize on the excuse of disappointment and eat it. But even my unbalanced mind understood that it would be nonsense to prejudice a fair trial, and it also occurred to me that, if I were to be really scrupulous, faith was enjoined. And although I had none and even found the word beyond my understanding, patience might be considered the next best thing. So I waited and the soup came.

As I finished it I heard the trolley approach a second time. Sometimes there was a surplus, which would be distributed round the cells in turn. This was an opportunity. The trolley came to within two cells of mine, but then there was a clattering of the empty cauldron and it was rolled away back to the kitchens.

This time the disappointment came near to breaking my resolve, and in a fit of temper I made for the corner where my bread was, to show my spite. But once more the new wisdom—perhaps it was simple canniness—halted me. Nothing more could happen on a Saturday, but just to defend myself I would have one side of the matter clear and wait till evening. Then the trial would have been fair and at least some result would have been achieved.

So I waited and forced myself to walk and to keep walking even when I heard the sergeants making the rounds of the floors, banging the keys in the locks to make sure that all was secure before they went to Paris. In all the week, it was the sound which I most dreaded, already knowing and feeling the silent featureless hours to follow, not only today but tomorrow also, and already counting the number of times I should have to walk up and down the cell before they would be past. But I succeeded, until heavy footsteps tramped down the landing and stopped outside my door.

Was this why Euripides called the Avenging Furies 'the Kindly Ones'? There was a horrid subtlety in such crude and simple irony, which seemed forever derisively to cap all acts of trust and all humility. 'Can a man be profitable unto God?' asked Eliphaz the Temanite. Was the answer 'No; but be careful to make sacrifices all the same, even without reward'? For once, I thought, I would have been right to eat my bread, for if a further interrogation was to be held I would need strength above all things.

But there was no time to dwell on the perversity of a fate which brought the Germans on this of all days to take me out. The key turned and the floor sergeant came in, followed by a monster *feldwebel* with a large gold tooth. The latter looked at me for a moment and then said:

'Your hair is too long.'

I said nothing, wondering that a sergeant-major could carry such fetishes even to the grave.

'Get it cut,' said the *feldwebel*, turning to the sergeant.

'*Jawohl!*' said the sergeant.

Carelessly, the *feldwebel* laid a slab of chocolate on the table, then, half-turning to go out, looked again as if appraising me and slowly laid another on the first. Then he muttered, '*Gut*', and went out.

The suspense which followed may be imagined. I stared and felt the chocolate in my hands for some time while my reason left me. Then, when it returned, as is the way with those who are attuned only to the rational order of things, I feverishly construed systems of logic which would explain the incident as ordinary. Perhaps this was a routine of which I did not know, a monthly dole which seemed marvellous in this first instance, but which later I would accept as a niggardly essential. Perhaps I had been condemned to death and this was some sort of last rite.

Yet the circumstances offered no encouragement to these ideas. The steps had come straight along the landing to my cell without stopping at others. It was unlikely that routine distributions would be made at this time, when the prison staff was eager to leave for the afternoon. Nor was the idea of secret condemnation congruous with that of special favour, at least not in terms of chocolate. Was this then the Prime Mover acting, as it were immediately? There was nothing illogical in the Prime Mover moving a *feldwebel* in the right direction; on the other hand, it was scarcely credible that this particular *feldwebel* had been so motivated.

With so little knowledge of what had happened, how could I justify such a terrible conclusion while there were other possibilities not yet disproved? Ideas of divine intervention would be so natural in a person who was physically prevented from seeing the natural causes that they would be for that reason suspect. The concept of the Feeder of Sparrows is too simple not to occur but it is also too simple to be easy to believe. But I did not pause long in subtle speculation. My mouth was watering, and I passed quickly from the Cause to the Effect.

Two slabs of chocolate, divided into ten bars each, made twenty bars. From then until Monday morning there would be about seventeen hours of daylight, in my reckoning of hours. I should therefore be able to eat one bar each hour for the whole weekend, and there would be three bars over. It would be unreasonable to start such severe rationing from the beginning, so I could eat the three bars at once, which would give me a good start and make discipline easier thereafter.

In ten minutes there were ten bars left, and in twenty, five. I watched them go quite objectively and observed with interest how the rivets of my resolution loosened one by one in relentless order and then dropped out, leaving holes thinly stopped by a putty of excuses which crumpled in turn and left the inner hollowness of my will exposed.

But when the five bars lay alone I stopped. Good intentions and a festive weekend were gone. I had not reckoned with my formidable appetite and would have shown a stronger mind by enjoying the chocolate as well as I could and, when it was gone, by thankfulness for small mercies. But to make amends I would keep the last bars until tomorrow, which would be as good a grace as was left to me.

I kept them in fact, but when I had eaten them I realized that I had not enjoyed them, and I thought later how foolish I had been to treat chocolate as a luxury to be gloated upon instead of as a food which I really needed. Had I done so, I might not have felt a twinge of suspicion that I was still being teased, pursued by irony, that I had been given a fish which had turned out in the end to have a serpent's tail.

But until my thoughts were overturned again by a third visit to the rue des Saussaies, I was fuller of joy and wonder than of doubt, and if sometimes an old spirit which had been sloughed off told me slyly that it would be better to accept life as it came with fortitude than to seek escapes from its hardships through magic suppositions (mere softening of the brain and heart), there seemed no more reason in its argument than in the other, and I was content with the humbler and more hopeful.

卌

Chapter 6

When the sergeant came for me this time he seemed to announce the withdrawal of the protective shield which I had wishfully imagined to be mine since the Saturday of the chocolate. He blew down my house of cards, but with less effect than before, as if I was sure that I could build it up again. Every morning and every night since the last interrogation I had repeated my story in detail and had tried to foresee and allow for its weak points, and I felt confident that by this evening I would have won the argument. During the journey in the van I went through a final rehearsal and was not anxious when I arrived.

A uniformed guard collected me from the van and led me up a wing of the building in which I had not been before. We stopped at an office, and the guard knocked, went in and muttered something, and then signalled to me to enter. A young man in plain clothes, with a rather soft face and wavy hair, rose politely and offered me his hand. For a moment I thought of ignoring it, thinking it wrong to compromise in the least degree with my enemies; but

83

rudeness seemed gross and even childish, so I shook the hand firmly but without enthusiasm and then sat in the chair which the other indicated to me opposite his desk. I studied him, found a high-domed brow and rather humorous un-German eyes, and foresaw truly that I had entered the intelligent phase in the cycle of interrogations.

The German made a few banal remarks by way of preface, probably to test the state of my nerves, and then said abruptly in his perfect French:

'So you say you are a prisoner-of-war? I will tell you at once that some people believe your story. But I'm afraid I don't. I know how easy it was and still is to cross the Pyrenees, and you cannot convince me that it was any more difficult for you than for others. Also we have, of course, found that the addresses you gave us in the south are non-existent. However, if you are not satisfied with my reasoning, I will ask you to go through the story again.'

Was it a double bluff? If I made no slip in the repetition, would he accept the story? I thought it unlikely and made a hasty review of the last line of defence, to which I should have to repair if this failed; but it was worth a good performance, and the process of re-telling, even if it were unsuccessful, would help to set the stage for the last act. So I went slowly through it, purposely omitting a detail here and there, which my opponent immediately pounced upon and demanded. And when I supplied an answer, there appeared first a puzzled, then an almost admiring, look in his eyes, which urged me to drive on and hammer in the wedge of doubt. But when I reached the end, he slowly put aside the statement from which he had been checking me and said:

'You play well, and I will continue this game with you. After you escaped from your division, you say you changed your clothes. Where?'

'At a farm. I couldn't tell you exactly where, though. I didn't know where I was at the time.'

'Well, we'll see if a map will help you. You apparently knew approximately in what area you were.' And he fetched from the adjoining room a large-scale map.

Now, I was confronted by two great difficulties at this point. First, I hardly knew, even generally, the geography of the area of Amiens, although I saw clearly enough that if I had been in action thereabouts I should be able to retrace my steps. Secondly, were I to succeed in a further bluff, and if my story were finally believed, the Germans would undoubtedly descend on the unfortunate farmer of my choice and punish him.

There was therefore only one solution. I must make a convincing display of map-reading, with all the necessary accompaniment of noises and head-scratching, and then ultimately become confused about the precise point at which I had changed my clothes.

Unfortunately my start was prejudiced, because the interrogator had carefully folded the map in such a way that neither Amiens nor any other place which might have given me my bearings was visible. Only the Somme, in winding blue, could be recognized, and I had but the vaguest notion of its course. But to confess ignorance was impossible and to unfold the map also, because he jealously held it, so with my finger I hunted diligently from place to place, snuffling at cross-roads and giving loud tongue at marshes and trigonometrical points, until suddenly my opponent gave a short laugh and opened the map to its full extent, allowing me to see that I had been remembering places many miles from the area in which I claimed to have been.

'You see?' he said, smiling faintly. 'I knew I was right. But now I want the truth.'

'But,' I protested, 'you can't expect me to read a map blind. I assumed that this'—pointing to a conspicuous road—'was the road from Amiens to St. Valéry. It certainly looks like it, and the country is all much the same around there.'

'Very well,' he replied; 'but you are wasting my time. I don't approve of the methods which were used on you last time, but if your duty is to keep your mouth shut, mine is to open it, and if it is necessary I will have to hand you back to the military, who are not likely to waste their time. But I will leave you for five minutes, and when I come back you will either show me that farm or tell me the truth.'

He went out, and a large ugly man in uniform came and stood over me. I kept my face turned towards the map so that he could not read my thoughts.

Although I had clearly been given leisure to use the map to any advantage and might easily have picked out my route on it, it was obvious that I would be subjected to the same test over the whole story and clear, at least to me, that sooner or later my pretence would be broken down. I was also firmly and fearfully convinced that a further interrogation by violence would bring the whole truth out of me, a fear reinforced by the physical menace of the knotty guardian leaning over me. Whether the fear of pain or the fear of self-disgrace was uppermost I do not know. They combined to lead me to one conclusion: that I must recant as a prisoner-of-war and produce an alternative story, which would be the last.

I had considered this situation from time to time and was convinced that the principles which I had used in the first instance were still applicable. It was necessary to convince the Germans at the outset that I had broken down and subsequently to tell them anything which would fit the facts known to them and maintain obscurity over those which they did not know.

I had not, however, thought very deeply about the details of a second story. The only thing of which I was reasonably sure was that the extent of their knowledge was strictly limited, and the task of filling in the two years of my life convincingly and without telling the truth after a mere five minutes' thought brought me to the verge of panic.

I let my eyes wander over the map to repose my mind, as seers watch tea-leaves or a crystal, and I kept saying to myself 'The Lord is my shepherd, therefore shall I lack nothing', but in the middle this changed to 'The Ford is my car'. There was no irreverence in this, but a reflection of the irony which I saw in all things. I needed the one version to be true, but I felt dreadfully aware that the other was more in keeping with my circumstances.

At length the interrogator came back and the big man went out.

'Well?' asked the former.

I kept my head bent and my voice (suitably, but by no means on purpose) unsteady.

'I shall have to tell the truth,' I said.

He sat down and rather kindly said nothing but gave me a cigarette. I was certain now that he had reckoned with my fear of torture.

After a little while he said:

'When you are ready, will you tell your story—the true one?'

'There's nothing much to tell now,' I said gloomily. 'I landed in France by parachute.'

'Well,' he smiled, feeling perhaps that kindness was the fruitful method. 'Let's keep things in order. What's your name?'

'All that I told last time,' I said, 'was true. At least in that respect. Everything up to 1940. You can check my name and so forth in directories if you take the trouble. But the last part is a bit different.'

I intended now to give him a military history with plenty of unimportant details which he could confirm, which would carry me through all the period of training and preparation and bring me to the eve of my arrival in France; thus I could safely feign ignorance over many matters. Had I been a prisoner-of-war I should have been guilty of saying too much, since the rule was to say nothing, but I had higher things at stake and felt free to discourse of my insignificant part in the Narvik campaign and the subsequent garrisoning of England. My questioner seemed to be bored with these matters, for he was no soldier and little interested in a soldier's deeds. But the plot still lay before him, and I brought him suddenly to it.

'On May fifteenth,' I said, 'I was sent for to report to the War Office.'

He brightened at once.

'What branch, and what was the name of the officer you saw?'

I gave him a room number and a name. Even if he knew them to be false he would not lay the falsification at my door but would realize that I myself would have been deceived.

'And what did he say?'

'He asked me if I would be prepared to go on a special mission to France.'

'And what did you say?'

I looked as ingenuous as I could.

'Well,' I said smugly, 'you can't say no to questions like that. Especially if it's not put as an order.'

'Quite. And then?'

'When I agreed, he told me to take a week's leave and then to go to the Midland Hotel at Manchester. I went there, and each day for a week I was fetched in a car and taken to an aerodrome where I was given parachute training.'

'What was the name of the airfield?'

'I was never told. It was some way to the north of the city.'

I had a rather delicate choice to make. We were in fact trained near Manchester, but to the south, and it was likely that if the Germans knew anything of us they would have located such an obvious centre. So I had to find a middle way between disclosing a place of which they might not know and destroying the credibility of the rest of my story, which was far more important, by telling an obvious lie about a matter of common knowledge. This was the solution I found on the spur of the moment. It was not a very happy one, falling between two stools, and many simpler answers occurred to me later, but the questions would not wait for my wits.

Meanwhile, my opponent studied my face closely and seemed to listen to my replies only with half his attention. From time to time he wrote with a little portable typewriter.

'And then?' he went on without comment.

'I went back to London and was given my instructions.'

'Did you see the same officer that time?'

'Him and another.' I gave another name. If my memory serves me truly the names I gave were those of marmalade-makers, because it was past breakfast-time.

'And what was your mission?'

'To find a man at Caen, give him some money and a message and to return.'

I was fortunately able to state with perfect truth that I could not describe the man since I had never seen him, but a photograph album was produced and I was asked if anybody in it corresponded to the description I had been given of him. The names were covered, but when the interrogator came to the picture I recognized from the one I had been shown, he let the cover slip so that I could see the name. But I passed on until eventually I came to a face largely concealed by bandages and said,

'That might be him, though it's very hard to tell.'

I was beginning to lose my confidence by this time. It was comparatively easy to invent stories concerning the English end of the matter, but the French side, and especially concerning people, was more difficult, because I could not be sure of the amount of evidence already available to the Germans. Of this man I knew nothing at all except that he had disappeared, and I assumed that he had either been arrested or had ceased to exist as himself; and I was afraid that if I made an obvious blunder in his case I would lose my way and ultimately betray Madame Terrien or Sébastien. But in fact I scarcely need have worried. He

89

had been arrested before I even arrived in France and spent the remainder of the war as a genuine prisoner-of-war, without any repercussions from my quarter.

Worse followed. The German delved into his pocket and pulled out the letter which I had written to Madame Terrien the night before my arrest and which I had never been able to post. Fortunately it was addressed to a mythical person at an accommodation address upon which we had agreed, and this offered me my chance, which I was not yet too stupid to forgo. He wanted to know all about this lady. I gave him a description of my sister, a meeting-place in a church to which she never went and a series of passwords which, if he used them with a forgery of my writing, would at once tell her of my arrest. It served its purpose, but not for long, for Madame Terrien and her children were all killed in our bombardment of Caen in 1944.

These details were carefully noted down on the little typewriter, and to my relief they seemed to be accepted, for my questioner changed the subject.

'And what was the message you were to deliver?' he asked.

'"Forget the Cherbourg line and go and find Yves."'

It was really the only intelligent reply I gave him. Whether it was a railway line or another kind and who was the mysterious Yves were secrets which had not been confided to my humble person, for my imagination had been content to leave the phrase rest on its laurels; and with the best will I could help him no further than he could himself. He came back on his tracks and worried me over details, but I had achieved my object and closed the circle of his questions. How was I going to return to England? The man in Caen would arrange it for me, and it was because I had not been able to find him that I was still in France.

The interrogator sometimes broke off his questioning and diverted me to other topics. Once he asked me whether I was not afraid that England would be Bolshevized as a result of our alliance with the Soviet Union. On another occasion he brought in a senior officer, a big grey man, to entertain me with personal remarks. I was a little cramped, however, by my temporary disability in German. Then, without warning he would snap a question at me.

'Were you ever at B—— ?' he asked once.

I was overjoyed.

'B—— ?' I said. 'Of course. I used to live very near it.'

'Where was that?'

'In Herefordshire.'

'But B—— is a long way from Hereford.'

'Not from my part,' I said. 'I'll show you on the map if you have one.'

He produced a map, and I showed him a B—— , differently spelled, in Worcestershire, whereas the one he meant was in quite another part of England. It was an easy victory and completely disarmed him. He spent some more time testing my story, but it was a simple weave and I could not lose the thread, and finally he made me sign the statement as he had written it.

It was late in the afternoon when he finally rang a bell and told an orderly to bring me a meal. It was a good meal of braised heart, which I remembered for many years after I had eaten it. When I had finished it, my interrogator drove me back to Fresnes in his own car. He talked little on the way, and of trivialities, but when we arrived at the entrance of the prison and a guard came out to take me, he held out his hand for a second time. 'Good-bye,' he said, 'I don't believe a word you've told me.'

𝍸 𝍷

Chapter 7

Soon afterwards the gales started to blow and swept from the stone prison such warmth as it had stored in summer. With them came another change, for the whole division, or wing, of the prison was transferred. (There were three long parallel divisions, of which we had been in the third, and this was now evacuated for women prisoners.) The move started at about midday and continued throughout the afternoon, and for some administrative reason the midday issue of soup was withheld. In the new chill I felt depressed and angry, stamping up and down my new abode in the insensate rage properly induced only in very young and thwarted children. When it was dark, coals of fire arrived in the form of a thick and warming mess of beans, of which we were given not only a full mess-tin but also a second helping. My spirit at once became soft with enjoyment and assured me that if I could rely on one such meal every three weeks or so I could survive in comfort. But such generous optimism lacked the support of the required condition and therefore soon subsided, leaving only the memory of one vast repletion to be compared odiously with the succeeding emptiness.

My new cell was identical with the old, or I should rather say that it had been built identically but had been tenanted by jail-birds of a lower order. The walls were splashed with dirt of many colours, the floor was chipped and rough, and, worst of all, the blankets were no more than rags. Those who live only with the barest elements of life are keen judges of their meagre assets and set great store by them, and the gloom of the dirt and the shreds of blankets boded worse for me than would the loss of a pair of shoes for a tramp. The old blankets had sufficed, as I had discovered by intricate experiment, to cover me, however barely; but the new ones, even with the most careful overlapping, could scarcely afford a single thickness of protection. I remembered being told that seventy- five per cent of a man's bodily heat was lost through exhalation, and I tried to evolve a way of sleeping in a tent. But however carefully I tucked it in it came continually undone.

I noticed, too, for the first time how thin I was becoming. My arms, for all the exercises I forced on them, were mere sticks, and I could already without difficulty pass my whole hand between my neck and the shirt collar which had once fitted. The cold was as yet no more than the first chill of autumn (we only call it freshness outside, after the summer) but I was shivering, and the prospect of winter gave me a short fit of anxiety which would have been hypochondria if there had been no cause for it. I had no clothes but a cotton shirt (thickened, it is true, by the dirt of continuous wear) and a serge suit of which the waistcoat was missing. My socks had been worn by the endless walking in loose unlaced shoes, so that there was no wool at all left on the soles, but only on the insteps and ankles. I once asked the sergeant for a new pair, but he only growled at me, and the same socks lasted until the following spring, when they disintegrated finally.

But if the spectacle of my own destitution took some of my

attention it seldom depressed me, except in my more perverse and theatrical moments, when I was feeling sorry and amused at myself as an old man exasperated at the absence of his favourite slippers; generally I felt the discomfort and let it pass, since I could do nothing for it. The bidding to consider the lilies of the field came to my mind continually, and I found that it leaves little room for revolt from circumstances. Consider them, indeed, and if you appear poor beside them there is only the plain fact to be observed that 'they toil not neither do they spin'; which accounts for no poverty but quietly rebukes all claim to wealth and silences complaint or the smugness of suffering without complaint.

I should not be truthful if I were to say that it replaced these things by some equivalent counterpart. Indeed, any such counterpart would have been too difficult for me to understand. The change in my outlook did not make me venture into faith, or even confidence; it did not occur to me that 'all these things shall be added unto you.' I had simply acquired a new ability to perceive that my own self was merely a small part of one creation. And I no longer felt that whatever blame I bore was of enough importance to bring the concentrated forces of the universe to bear exclusively against me.

More intricate patterns and relationships could be vaguely discerned beneath the surface of habitual appearances, and I was slowly and unconsciously coming to accept that my impotence and littleness could attract a support to which my erstwhile self-importance could never have aspired.

This change came quietly, so that I was almost unaware of it except in moments of rebellion. The simple acknowledgment of a minor planet that it is not, after all, the sun does not greatly alter its customary gyrations, although it may perform them with more grace, and the subtle persuasion to the same effect which had come upon me did not drive me to prayers and prostrations which were foreign to my nature, nor to expectations which went against the grain of my habitual view of the nature of things. I remembered the afternoon when the *feldwebel* had brought me chocolate, but I remembered it with awe and was afraid of rather than impatient for a repetition of that happening. Miracles were still matters of fable for me, and I would as soon have seen Red Riding Hood's grandmother appear as the doors of my cell open. But I accepted the likelihood of timely help, even without miracles.

Moreover, whenever it occurred to me to presume that this state of, as it were, dependence should logically bring results of the kind suggested by the Prodigal Son, it happened that the thought was born only to be proved false.

One morning when I was feeling particularly cold and wondering where I should find the energy to shiver, I remembered the saying, 'God tempers the wind to the shorn lamb.' It was a comforting thought, and I began to visualize the sergeant bringing me an extra blanket or doubling my rations. But shortly afterwards the barber appeared and sheared off my hair. It was too pointed to be treated as a casual annoyance. If the rations had been small or some other trivial discomfort had been inflicted, I might have felt wronged. As it was I could only repeat to myself the proverb I had remembered, but with rather more philosophical assertion than before.

Having in this way relinquished my illusion of being the pivot and focus of all things, I found that the imminence of death was less oppressive than before. Perhaps this was partly because I had no further decision to make in the matter. I had taken the last step open to me and was therefore relieved of the need to consider evasion, which is the most exhausting part of all apprehension. Also, no doubt, such a fear cannot live long with a man without stirring his contempt.

I was nervous in the early mornings, which I assumed to be the time of convocation, and gave thanks each evening for having survived another day. Each day I recited my story, to keep it fresh, but I found passages which I could no longer confirm and began to believe that I had in fact given everything away and that the story I believed I had told was only that which I had wished to tell. A Chinese proverb has it that 'where there is much talking, there is surely some scandal', and I spent hours doubting, trying to remember what scandal lay at my door and with what words I had betrayed my friends. But there were no sources but my unruly memory and peevish doubt, and I have still only the evidence that my friends survived long after my arrest to suggest that I had succeeded at least in some measure. Finally, I was attacked sometimes by a vicarious sadness for my mother, for my younger brother had been reported missing in a submarine in February, and she would now have no news of me at least until France was retaken. But I was free of any temptation to brood and no longer found myself scrabbling to free myself from my cage.

Autumn went its way unruffled by impatience on my part. I had not yet learned to count in months and years and was content to live day by day, filling them mostly with memories of rainy hills and London's damp dark evenings and the pale sunlight catching the pastel stone of Paris. (I could see them through the walls, and each had its earthy counterpart of food and drink.) And for exercise and discipline I had my *bourgeois* bread-hoarding, which I despised for its pettiness but held to for its profit both to my nerves and to my night-time comfort. But the spark of rebellion was still alight in me, and in one respect at least I claimed jurisdiction over my future.

'One thing,' I assured myself, 'is out of the question. I cannot still be here at Christmas.'

The possibility occurred to me some time before the event, and I dismissed it at once as absurd and unthinkable. My way of life alone would prevent it, for if I was not shot or released or transferred soon I should undoubtedly go mad, but even if none of those things were to happen it was still impossible. I do not think I was normally more than an average enthusiast for Christmas, but now I counted all its attributes of rejoicing, of reunion, of kindness and feasting, and decided that Fresnes and Christmas were quite incompatible. As the day drew nearer, I became sentimental about it, wondering how best to spend it there; but still, when it arrived, I would not be there. This was an axiom.

In the afternoon of December 18 the door of my cell opened, and a young man came in, dressed in a dark suit and carrying a briefcase. Thinking him a Gestapo man, I was for a moment both alarmed and surprised that he should have come here rather than have me sent to him. But he advanced into the cell and said in very German French:

'I am the Protestant padre. I have seen in the register that you are not a Roman Catholic.'

I was taken aback and said nothing, not too ready to believe him, for the Gestapo were by no means above using such a trick. I offered him my stool but he declined and sat on the bed, while I perched on the hinged table.

'I only came to tell you', he said, 'that if you want to receive Holy Communion I can obtain permission for you. Would you like that?'

I was still more astonished at these words and sensed an unwelcome implication in them.

'Do you mean as last rites?' I asked him. 'As a matter of fact, I don't think it would be possible, because I have never been confirmed.'

'I don't think that would matter,' he replied; 'but I have not come for that reason. Have you been condemned?'

I told him that I did not know but that I would not be surprised to learn of it.

'These things are difficult,' he said. 'But I have no doubt it will be all right. Anyway, I can assure you that I have come only as a matter of routine. I visit all the non-Catholics, because all

98

prisoners are allowed to receive the Communion if they wish unless there is some special restriction against them.'

Now I had decided that I wanted to talk to him, but I found that the muscles of my mouth had become stiff and unwilling and that the thoughts and questions I had wanted to express became ridiculous when I turned them into words.

For months I had allowed my thoughts to run freely and deeply, unhampered by the need to convey them to another person or by the delicacies and conventions of speech which normally keep our tongues insulated from our inner selves, and now that I would have liked to test them I was unable to voice them. How could I ask this ordinary little man, composed and dutiful, whether the parable of the Prodigal Son was to be taken literally and whether there was any reason why I should not apply it to myself? How should I set about applying it? Wasn't it perhaps a perfectly normal refuge for people in my circumstances, a sort of wishful escape without any foundation in fact?

I was appalled at the thought of the answers I would get: that it was not in our power to say how God would work, that all parables were true but, being parables, they were not always to be taken literally; and so forth. I was not prepared for such a conversation.

'It's very kind of you,' I said, my lips feeling as if they were frozen hard, 'but when you are in the sort of position I am in, ceremonial does not seem very important, although other things are. It would even be hypocritical for me, because I should be doing something I have never done before and don't really believe in.'

Then I went on rather rudely:

'I think really I shall have to solve my religious problems in my own mind, but you may be able to explain one thing to me. I assume that a Christian would say that my present condition is a punishment, which is easy to understand. But if I'm being punished for things I have done, why do other people get punished through me for what they haven't done?'

I said this rather belligerently, but he was quite unruffled.

'I don't think we could claim to explain that,' he said. 'After all, people have so many things which are secret that we don't know enough about them to explain why things happen to them.'

He got up from the bed and fumbled in his briefcase.

'Perhaps I can't help you now,' he said, 'but if you want to see me you can always ask and I shall come if I can.' And he handed me a sheet of paper.

I felt that I had been crude and smiled as well as I could to show him that I was sorry if I had hurt his feelings. Then he left me, a little angry with myself but making the excuse that I was not sure that he was what he claimed to be.

And when he was gone I wanted to bring him back, for I at once became able again to frame the questions which I wanted answered. I was like a man worried that he has a cancer and determined at long last to declare his symptoms to a doctor, but who, when a doctor comes, complains weakly of swollen tonsils and lets him go. I was not worried but baffled by the numberless and paradoxical conclusions which could be drawn from any one of the comforting assurances of the Gospel.

Being naturally and circumstantially inclined to favour a literal interpretation of straightforward passages about sparrows and lilies and lost sheep, I found myself hardly reconciled with less optimistic exhortations to wait for the other world. And from what I could remember of the sermons I had heard, there was a general attitude of warning among churchmen that the benefits of Providence were not to be counted upon on earth, in the form of material comforts, but in an intangible experience after death.

Since I was growing daily more uncomfortable and less aware that I must die, this interpretation was of little use to me and struck no response in either heart or mind; the whole Gospel became more and more a structure of paradoxes, carefully balanced so that each statement could be invalidated by another, none having absolute precedence. The lost sheep, the foolish virgins; the prodigal son and the man with one talent: they made an impenetrable maze through which I could see no way. But the opportunity to ask was past.

I picked up the sheet which the padre had left, a little excited, because whatever it contained it was something to read and therefore something to pass a little time. It was in the form of a sermon and for title bore a text from one of the Psalms: 'For all our days are passed away in Thy wrath; we spend our years as a tale that is told.' I thought that the second phrase must be the best description ever given of a prisoner's life. For a few moments we sat in our discomfort, with the words of our stories echoing in our ears. Like musicians who have played their piece, we would remain silent and motionless for a space before leaving. Then 'the place thereof shall know it no more.' But the theme of what followed was the anger of God and the frailty of human life to withstand it; and I was outraged at the representation of God as a ferocious scourge when I was almost convinced that He was kind. I regretted no longer the shallowness of my conversation with the padre, feeling that if he could propagate such an offensive idea in print we would surely have found no common ground for speech. The God portrayed in this interpretation was of no use to me, for wrath (*courroux* was the French word, quicker and testier than the English) indicated such an uncertainty of temper as could hide mercy only by accident; and this was pessimism, which, in such a place at least, was death. Nevertheless, I read the pamphlet for hours, until I knew it by heart, and the speeches and arguments which I worked up against it occupied me for a long time afterwards and saved me from stagnation.

Four days later another interruption brought me back to immediate reality. A strange sergeant came to my cell and told me to collect my things, of which I had none, and ordered me out of the door. For once I was not paralysed, though I felt cold when I discarded the blanket I had been wearing as a cloak, and I asked him where I was going more out of curiosity than of fear.

He was unusually communicative.

'Down to the second floor,' he said. 'This floor will be used to put three or four prisoners in a cell, so you are being moved down.'

'Do you know why they don't move others in with me?' I asked, as we walked down the stairs.

'Police orders,' he said shortly, and this seemed to him sufficient explanation.

Cell No. 239 was no different from the others, but I had the same feeling of being uprooted as if I had been living for a long time in a warm Georgian house and had had to move to a draughty villa. Yet, when I had examined the appointments of my new home, I found much to recompense me for the change. The floor was shiny, the cement round the lavatory was clean and not yet crumbling and, best of all, the blankets were new, full-size and with all their hair. The plug pulled, the tap flowed, and there was even a pane of transparent glass in the skylight, which gave me many square inches of extra light and extra sky to look at. It was wonderful to look at the sky, whatever the weather. Little clouds lit like southern islands in the sunset, or fast grey scurries, or the blue fullness of invisible things were all beauty to me. I knew why we put Heaven up there, and could not tire of looking at it.

The worst feature of the change appeared in the floor-staff. It seemed that the authorities had determined that the prisoners in solitary confinement were the more dangerous, and they had wished on us a trio of guards of an unpleasantness to daunt even the least faint-hearted. The sergeant looked as if a witch had tried to turn a gnome into a toad. The transmutation had been arrested half-way and had left the two sets of features in the one diminutive body: bulging eyes, vast, down-turned mouth, crapulousness, wrinkles, and a sub-human peevish cunning which ever drove him to spy on us silently from behind our shoulders. He had a deep hoarse croak, and if there were no warts visible on the exposed portions of his skin, they were not lacking in his spirit.

Two corporals were his apprentices, one a simple bat-eared bruiser with a strong neck supporting a head which undoubtedly contained the overflow of his muscle, the other more dangerous, because he had strength neither in his mind nor in his body.

He looked mild and inoffensive and seldom shouted, but warred on us with sneak-thief weapons, cutting the soup ration and reporting us to the Toad.

I received their several and unwelcome visits shortly after taking up my new residence. They were out to persuade me of my iniquity and their *force majeure*, the Toad and the bruiser blustering and barking and the little one prying silently for dust. They wanted me to stand at attention immediately they entered, but I managed to teach them that my movements were slow and my positions languid.

From upstairs I heard the unremitting roar of the old sergeant and felt almost homesick. '*August! August! Wo ist der Mann? Verfluchter August!*' Then a little chirrup from some distant corner, and: '*Komm, Mann! Geh mal Brot holen!*' And, sadly: '*O-je, dieser August!*'

August was no longer mine, but I had new blankets.

𝍸𝍸 𝍩

Chapter 8

Christmas was snow-white and cold. My change of cell had kept my mind off it for four days, and it was only on Christmas Eve that I realized fully that the paradox had become truth and that I was after all still there. All that evening I wandered up and down in my blanket-cloak, sensing the snow outside and listening to the choirs of German soldiers singing carols, the voices coming to me like a single voice, purified by the snow. I assured myself that there was still time, that anything was possible except the one event which I had excluded. But my assurances only served to convince me that I was wrong and that probably I had made it necessary for me to be wrong by setting the limit in the first place. I recalled the old injunction to beware of tempting Providence and assumed that I had broken the rule. But then, I thought, did the temptation of Providence mean so much? I had believed it to mean that Providence should not be defied to do something which you either wished or feared; I had not realized that it meant that one should never, on any subject, presume that a certain thing would happen however benign and innocent. By the time I went to bed I was properly humbled.

When I woke to the Day itself I made one final and histrionic protest to myself, but to a sceptical and somewhat laconic self which quite illogically assured its other half, the play-acting one, that if I had been wrong about Christmas I would be right about some other day. And it immediately proceeded to set that other day as Easter. Christmas, it said, was an unreasonable time for anything to happen, at least in Europe, but in spring the snows would melt in Norway and the tides rise higher in the Channel, and there would almost certainly be an invasion of the Continent then. St. Nazaire had been in the spring, and Hitler had waited for it in 1940, and it was in every way preferable to the late summer, when harvests were interrupted and the autumn rains too close ahead.

In the end, I spent a large part of that fateful day in a state of statistical hypnosis, confidently calculating the time needed to make a tank and a landing-craft, and deciding in the end that spring would be the time and I would not be here at Easter. Looking back, I thought that my four months had been easily passed and I was not dismayed by the consideration that they would now be doubled. The essential, though I did not know it consciously at the time, was to have a boundary which would make time finite and comprehensible, but my sagacious self also let it be hinted that if I chose a date so far ahead, I would placate Providence and perhaps have my impotence in the matter proved by being delivered almost immediately. I began to watch the moon diligently through my good pane of glass, so that I could anticipate the higher and the lower tides.

Little moments of wonder were interspersed among all this sorcery. Being apart from the celebration of Christmas, I was able to see more comprehensively the picture of millions of people being happy on one particular day. I could see them all, spread out over the world, unable to see each other, not all of them, perhaps, happy but all moved by the same necessity for happiness, from children ecstatic with their miraculous stockings, to old solitaries escaping for a moment with shy gifts and reluctant greetings.

Was it only a tradition, kept with the aid of a calendar and the advertisements of shops, that led to this outburst? Four hundred million Chinese did much the same at their New Year; in what were they different? Was the difference important or the likeness, the tradition or the joy? Even if one creed were better than another, it did not follow that the rejoicing was better on that side, because so few people really understood a creed. So rejoicing alone appeared enough. Perhaps the human race was saved if it could be happy once a year, even without, belief.

This was a Friday, and when the Toad appeared alone on duty and in his best uniform, I understood that we would have a weekend of three days. I would sooner have had the company of the noise of prison business than the cold silence, but I felt that the God of Wrath had been dispelled again, and with my new calculations to absorb me the day was soon gone and the next term opened.

卌 Ⅲ

Chapter 9

The days between Christmas and Easter are as alike as drops of water, uniformly bleak and uneventful, as if winter had wiped the character from them as oratory wipes it from a crowd. New Year's Day itself is only a mimic, and often a tired one when it has been properly brought in. The rest follow each other in obscurity, claiming none of our attention and defying the worthy enthusiasts who tried to brighten them with St. David and St. Patrick and the mysterious Lady Day. Probably I had chosen Easter as my new horizon because it was the first feature to be seen across this twilit desert.

Left to itself, nature follows the lead, and each person and animal and plant is reduced by winter to its smallest limits, living as nearly within itself as it can do while time takes a brief holiday from the rhythm of succession. Blizzard and storm hustle the restless into shelter, frost orders them into the torpid comfort of the heaviest blankets, and the monotony firmly rebukes distraction and allows mind and body to chew fatly on their cud.

Hibernation is a blessing which we have almost circumvented in our whimsical way.

At Fresnes, of course, the passage of these days seemed less benign than nature had intended. The climate was not tempered by our blankets, which soon proved their ersatz origin, and the monotony was not stillness but itching impatience for the first sign of that interminably distant spring which would warm us and bring our rescue nearer. Instead of warm somnolence we had cold and pinched anxiety. Each day's soup convinced us that we could not live on stuff so thin, and each night we faced our beds with reasoned pessimism, like sailors cast away in an arctic sea. But each morning we survived to watch our small skies for the approach of clemency, and we listened for familiar sounds of life as children listen for their parents' voices late at night.

Yet the season would not be quite denied. The pittance of diversion, which had been in the humming of summer and the windy bustle of autumn, was gone. The endless walking up and down had to be interrupted more and more often by intervals of sitting or lying tightly wrapped, head and all, in the blankets, when, in concentrated immobility, a little time of warmth could be achieved. (With practice, I could maintain a state almost of anaesthesia for perhaps half an hour at once.) And at such times the mind was more detached and calmer even than when oscillating absently over a pair of plodding feet; and memory found only rare excerpts from the nameless winter days of other years, because they, too, had been an immersion rather than a measured flow and not broken up by incidents.

On the other hand, I found a new activity, which was more enervating but seemed more useful than promenading. My straw mattress was filled with oat-straw, and I found that many of the oats had been left over from the threshing. I decided to eat them and spent many hours collecting, husking and amassing them in a little pile. When this seemed to be a small mouthful (perhaps twice a day if I worked hard), I ate it with due ceremony, thinking a little smugly that God helped those who helped themselves.

Such glib quotations were becoming habitual to me. I did not understand nor consciously believe them, but they emerged spontaneously, like clichés overheard a thousand times and dismissed as often, flitting in and out with the familiarity of accustomed residents, appropriate to the inclination of my thoughts, but coming to them as no more than decoration. Yet they provoked me to meditation.

My religious education (if it can be called that) had been so conducted as to make it resemble an algebra class as much as possible. Neither subject seemed worth learning at that age unless it were given a rigorously down-to-earth and practical significance; the dead languages were endowed with more of both beauty and narrative interest. God was given a place corresponding to the zero on the right hand of an equation, an unexplained but convenient symbol of which the manipulation could produce solutions as required; and various generalities, such as sin, were introduced as occasion demanded but with as little clarity as the square root of minus one.

Later, when the world widened and my faculties were busy sampling it, religion and algebra were consigned to the same limbo of dismal textbooks. Algebra remained a handy way of measuring stair-carpets, and religion kept vaguely pointing upwards, available as an occasional reference-system for the weighing of behaviour.

I have heard it said that the Jesuits can preach to any kind of person, from a farm-hand to a physicist, and suit their words to each and all, while other preachers can only make themselves understood to their own kind.

We were taught as befitted grandsons of Victorians and the heirs, willynilly, of Cromwell; and we acquired a code of rules for our conduct which should help us to be good servants of our country. It drew some colour, no doubt, from the New Testament, but it was not in substance more authentically Christian, or religious in any way, than the similar codes of Spartans and Persians, Japanese and Teutons. The points of detail and of ritual differed, and circumstances produced different particular results, but the essential conception of nobility was fairly universal, and, as Professor A. N. Whitehead pointed out, even the wheeling rooks have their ritual. It was a good code, exhorting us to honesty, co-operation and self-sacrifice, but it was useful only to a free and active man, with goals to reach and responsibilities to carry. I wished I had followed it more strictly while I was free, but goals were futile now and my last responsibility was past. I was passive, motionless; and a code of behaviour has no bearing on that condition.

The other recollections of my scriptural days were no more helpful. There were the everlasting Don'ts of Moses, the primness of St. Paul, the starchiness of vicarage teas and the tart recriminations of schoolmasters who donned gowns on Sundays.

Then there was 'religion', which was not part of the lesson but which underlay it tacitly, an unmentionable which was only rarely blurted out by an unfortunate text or a stray visiting preacher. It seemed to be a positive aspect of Christianity and a stumbling-block, concerning people who did good things while the normal population simply avoided doing bad, precluding enjoyment and being the special function of monks. Any man, I presumed, who became devoutly religious should honestly become a monk. The logic is not uncommon, because a convention to that effect has reigned long enough to pass almost without question; and many of us would add, not the converse, that the monk is a religious man, but the corollary, that because the monastic life is impracticable to all but a few, so must religion be forbidden to ordinary men.

From my cell, I could accept this reasoning with conviction, for the thought that I should spend the rest of my life with no better home could not be entertained. It was, I thought, not better, but a matter of no choice that I should die an unconverted sinner and take my chance with the judgment rather than condemn myself outright to such an existence. If solitude and frugality were the monk's portion, then let him have them. I wanted the world, sinful or pure, as long as there was a square meal left in it and room to kick my heels.

I have mentioned how I was given paper. Sometimes it consisted of old newspapers torn up, sometimes of the pages of books, and, depending on the corporal who issued it, I would get a few sheets or a small book at one time. I now had a series of pages from books which had evidently been sent by charitable societies for our spiritual refreshment but which had been turned by the Germans to the baser use, and from them the last pages of a book about St. Francis of Assisi were impressed firmly in my mind. The passage described with an almost voluptuous insistence the joy of contemplating the saint's impoverished life and particularly the dusty garbage which he ate from his bowl.

I suspected that the author preferred to take his pleasures vicariously and I drew in effigy a well-nourished friar dropping unctuous verbiage on sore souls from whose troubles he was himself majestically protected. No man, I felt, who had experienced the reality could write such tartuffian nonsense. I could leave Puritania without a backward glance, but not change it for a monastery. Wherever I looked, this Christianity was marked by a Dickensian darkness and a thinness of lip and a voice which called for suffering and yet more suffering. Were all these things pleasing to a God of Love?

I was afraid that if I had the choice between good living and asceticism I should choose the former, whatever the consequences, but I regretted that such a choice should be unavoidable. Hope, alone and unreasoning, had led me to expect that there was room for belief in the kindly things of the Gospel, but since apparently Wrath held the balance, I should have to abandon hope.

113

It would not be abandoned, but the subject was too confused in my mind for me to inspect it further. Fortunately, the passions are good governors of the intellect, bringing it back to firm ground when it takes flight from gravity; and as even the purest mathematicians have sometimes to grope for a solid hand-rail, so my stomach, the faithful beast, offered me an earthly refuge whenever my thoughts became unsafe. They did not often reach great heights, for hunger is no aid to concentration, and my only source of thought was my memory—not wise memory, as Carlyle spoke of, working with wise oblivion, but a palette from which emerged an untidy kaleidoscope of image and association, diverting but seldom constructive.

And if sometimes I believed that I had been thinking intelligently, it was only to find a greater perplexity beyond, to which I could no longer bring my wits to bear. Then my stomach resumed its errand of mercy, and I dreamed of old meals. Thought was like the stone of Sisyphus and wistful lunacy the symbol of contentment.

Indeed, I felt less sane after these weeks than ever before, and my condition was not improved when a bell suddenly started to toll the hours. It was a disaster of truly great proportions. The bell was cracked and made a dreadful sound of pain and ugliness, a note without rhythmic frequency, against all the laws of nature. It also multiplied the days, for instead of two periods of waiting, from dawn to soup and from soup to nightfall, there were now twenty-four, each one as long as ever.

The bell never told of progress, never gave a sudden surprise by announcing that the day was farther gone than I had thought. Indeed, it seemed to preface every stroke by a sarcastic 'it's only...' Then the same jinx which had inspired the mechanism to move took to tinkering with it, and the quarter-hours started to sound, in one, two and three notes, each one obscenely discordant from the others, until finally slapstick replaced comedy, and the hours and quarters clanged out witlessly at intervals of five, ten, or a hundred minutes, sometimes two or three in succession.

When the toneless and unmeasured beating of the clapper came across the night, its dissonance sharpened by the cold, and woke me in the small hours from my precious sleep, it could twist my brain like a dentist's drill; and when it stopped its first movement I was so anxious not to hear the next that I was unlikely to go to sleep again. At last, as suddenly as it had started, it became dispossessed of its devil and we had silence again. But for weeks afterwards I listened nervously for it to return.

One day, towards the end of winter, while I was husking oats, the Toad caught me unawares through the peep-hole, stormed furiously in and asked me what I was doing.

'*Essen*,' I said; '*gut!*' And he, for once dumbfounded, screwed a short forefinger in his temple and withdrew, muttering, leaving me to my peaceful husbandry.

Perhaps he was right, for either the raw and ancient oats or the official food smote me with some kind of dysentery as the spring arrived. It was a nauseating disease and the more exasperating for its apparent ability to live on nothing. For a few days I suffered it in silence, wondering from what copious hidden springs it drew its restless poisons, but one morning I reported it to the corporal who delivered the morning paper, not because I relied on him to attend to it but because I could live with it no longer, like a man who hides lice for a while with instinctive shame, but afterwards finds himself forced to share his embarrassment with others.

My plight stirred an unexpected sympathy in the corporal, or perhaps it was only the horror which disease inspires in Germans, and he produced a medical orderly who, in turn, prescribed charcoal and starvation. He gave me a little heap of charcoal balls, like duck-shot, which were sweet and crunchy. I ate them gladly as an addition to the ordinary diet, but the command to eat nothing else fell on deaf ears, for he might as sensibly have told me to stop breathing. I could feel acutely that the bread, especially, was sour and an irritant, but wisdom had once again to bow before appetite. The dysentery lingered for a few weeks and then suddenly disappeared, probably from exhaustion.

卌 ‖‖

Chapter 10

Spring was announced by a blackbird, who chose a platform close outside my window and sang loudly and tempestuously of hope and love and the freedom of the new earth. I told myself stories in the same tenor, in tune with the spirit of the season, so that the blackbird became Sullivan to my Gilbert. But when I remembered, seeing the window and its bars between me and the sun and air, that his world was real and mine a shadow, I wished that he would seek partnership elsewhere. Then, one day, I was let out for exercise.

The prison, as I have told, was composed of three great parallel blocks of cells. The spaces in between seemed like canyons, and it was here that the exercise yards had been built. Along each side of the canyon was a line of little courtyards, each about ten yards square and surrounded by walls of overgrown red brick. They were like miniature Elizabethan gardens, forgotten and nestling together for company under the towering concrete. They were deep in grass and weeds, and the walls were encrusted with little plants and inscribed with salutations, boasts and threats by earlier outlaws whose language, if not Elizabethan, stemmed straight from Rabelais. A brick path, buried in the green undergrowth, was laid in a square following the walls, and along the whole row was a cat-walk from which sentries, dispelling the illusion, could overlook the inmates.

Fifteen of us were let out at one time. As soon as the preceding group was safely back, our doors were opened one by one and, with a good interval between us to keep us from talking, we were driven downstairs with a barrage of shouts: '*Heraus! Los, los! Schnell! Pass auf! Fresse halten! Los!*' The corporals and sergeants of all the floors, and even the warrant officers downstairs, took up the senseless din, to marshal our descent and prevent us from closing to exchange a greeting or a glance. Only the furtive sentries, with their rifles and oversized grass slippers, remained silent.

My cell was at the corner of the stairs; No. 238 went before me and No. 240 after me. The former was separated from me by the stairway and meant little to me, in the sense that the character of our neighbours was known only in so far as we could interpret their or the enemy's activity next door. He was too far away for any trace of his existence to have reached me, and solitude had so far weaned me from the habit of intercourse, even the thin intercourse of speculation, that I could no longer see any relationship with another person unless it were introduced gradually by a long overture of common trivialities. So No. 238 remained forever only a human back for me.

Even of No. 240, of whom I knew comparatively much, I can remember little, except that he was young and grey of face and anxious to talk. He had tried to involve me in the tapping game and to bribe me with news (for he was only recently captured) in order to lure me into conversation and, perhaps, commiseration. But I had no patience for this pastime, which was tedious and unreliable and eased none of the real burdens of confinement, and I had finally given up the pretence of answering after I learned that a general named Eisenhower was on the point of winning the war for us in the Mediterranean. Having never heard the name, I assumed it to be German and thought that my neighbour was confusing the issues of the war. After that I replied to his overtures with a few deceitful knocks to assure him that I was listening and resumed my pacing and my own thoughts, which were by now more congenial to me than rumours.

As we went downstairs I heard No. 240 shuffle up behind me and whisper urgently, '*Pourquoi tu ne réponds plus?*' But before I could even think of a sensible answer a lurking sergeant had barked a warning at him and he had drawn back. Then No. 238 turned into his courtyard, a back without identity, recorded like a minute of some past year on a clock-face, an indistinguishable occurrence; and feeling for a moment in myself the same remote quality of irrelevance, I too turned aside, and the door slammed and locked behind me.

For all the studied segregation there was a great whistling and chattering all around, to which the sentries on the cat-walk paid but fitful and benign attention. It was often a surprise and something of a relief to find that the humbler among our oppressors were prone to embarrassment rather than to bullying and tried, with uniform inaction, to avoid our hatred and their masters' fury at the same time. Now gossip bubbled over.

'What's your name? When were you arrested? Where? Why? Did you get a parcel this week? I'll throw you a cigarette over the wall. The new corporal is in the artillery and has just come back from Russia.' And then the inevitable tale of victory.

I listened for a while, finding the voices strange and delightful in their way, but having no wish to join them. I wanted to enjoy the newly-discovered things about me and would have preferred to be alone to absorb the sky and grass and air, so that I felt a faint resentment at the noise and a fear that one of my neighbours would waste some of my precious minutes by talking to me, like those people who insist on whispering in concerts. But my tongue was securely tied, and perhaps it was better that the new world was kept human in its due proportion.

The renewing of old acquaintances, and especially of cherished ones, often begins with a touch of perverse humour. An oddity will strike the eye before any well-remembered feature; 'What funny shoes', we will say, or 'I never knew her mouth was crooked'. Under the cover of a momentary strangeness the urbane sub-conscious mind has one wry look before admiration shuts it out.

So, when the door had shut behind me, the first thing of which I was conscious was the wall of the opposite building. I noticed that the shadow which served as my clock in the morning was cast by an eave of the red-tiled roof, and that the depth and angle of this eave were such that the shadow would grow very slowly in the early hours but quite rapidly as the zenith approached. I noted, therefore, that I need not be impatient in the early morning but must guard against over-optimism towards midday. I also noted that such an observation was in fact of no account, because it was too early for me to judge the turning-point and anyway I should always err on the side of impatience, however precise I became in my time-keeping.

Meanwhile, my feet were recognizing the strange but well-loved feeling of treading on soft turf, and my eyes and nose were engaged in their own rediscoveries of life. Although I was in the canyon, the enormous sweep of the sky was overwhelming, and the light coming from all directions instead of through a window gave everything a startling brilliance. Perhaps best of all was the careless way of the growing grass, short here, long there, facing in all directions, and with dandelions spreading darker patches waywardly where their seed had dropped. An abandoned plot, it would be called; in England someone would be told to plant cabbages in it; but to me it was Arcadia. ('I guess it is the handkerchief of the Lord,' said Walt Whitman.) I walked around it, avoiding the brick path which had no business there, and felt the air, suddenly warm and throbbing, pouring life into me as it did into the grass.

And knowing that the time would be short, I tried to store it all in my mind, to imbue myself with it as a proof against my cell, as I might drink rum before leaving a sinking ship. But it would not be captured. The clatter and shouting started again and the doors were opened and I wondered whether to take my last look at the sky or at the grass. I picked a small snail off the wall to serve as a companion and as a memorial. Then we resumed our shuffling back to the third floor.

Back in my cell, I put the snail on the table and tried to recall the sensations of outside. But they would not come back, and I spent the rest of the morning frustrated, concentrating on smells and sights and feelings which would not come of their own selves now that the physical forms in which they travelled were excluded.

When the soup came, I gave the snail little pieces of cabbage, but they did not seem to strike its fancy. It stayed for one night, but disappeared during the second. When it had gone, I told myself that I had been ridiculous in bringing it back with me, but it was company of a sort, and as it were an emissary from the world of real life; and its going reminded me of freedom, even suggesting that what a snail obtained so easily might still be possible for me.

For a few days I waited impatiently to be let out again. My little sky was no longer enough, and when I remembered the warmth of the air I realized that I was still shivering, even though wrapped in a blanket. But although nothing further happened, I could not live through the spring without gladness: I did not feel in duty bound to be happy, as Wordsworth once did; I could not help it. Now I liked to wake early and listen to the blackbird singing and think about daffodils and budding silver birches and what I was doing last spring and all the springs before, *laudator temporis acti se puero.*

The word 'love' inevitably occurred to me, but since it did not touch my now tenuous emotions and caught in my memory only the shadows of sadness, I saw it as a strange word of which I did not know the meaning and began to dissect and ponder it.

I was at once thrown into confusion by my untimely and remorseless memory, which reminded me that one should love one's enemies. Time and the change of season had damped the doubts and paradoxes which had beset me earlier, and I was well disposed to see the world ruled by kindness. But 'love your enemies' seemed to have no meaning. The idea of loving the Toad or his minions repelled me almost as strongly as had the thought of monasticism, and it was abundantly clear that here was an obscurity in my understanding upon which, again, nobody had yet cast light.

I did not hate my enemies. I would do what I could to frustrate their schemes against me, but I would not be savage with them. If the Toad would go back to Germany and leave my door open, he could go in peace; I would try to neutralize his unpleasantness, but I would not harry him to hell. But the Toad and love seemed to be incompatible terms. It would be easy enough to couple them in church, especially in the general proposition, an exhortation given in peculiarly suitable circumstances where outright refutation or even doubt would be unlikely. For in those peaceable surroundings the vision of enmity recedes. But does the vision of love advance? Do we know what we are talking about?

We use the word happily of wives and children, food and old coats, golf and barley sugar: is there any meaning in the word which can be common to our relations with all these things? Does it represent a single identifiable happening? There is no one concept of love, however many symbols may be invented for it. If you see or hear the word, it may provoke a variety of memories of objects or persons with whom it has been associated, but nothing in all the thought around it can be isolated and identified as itself. Poets mirror love roughly in refractory words; philosophers skirt round it in wide detours; and if more lyrics have been sung than doctrines expounded on it, that is no doubt because lyrics are brief and pleasing and doctrines interminably long. Yet we never abandon the subject, since our minds, split between soul and sense, are forever seeking to explain intuition by reason and to enjoy reason by salting it with intuition.

Knowledge is always increasing, and because knowledge comes from inspection and analysis the size of things known seems to decrease as the number of things known grows. The words we use multiply, but the scope of their application becomes more rigidly precise: as we learn to split hairs we find less use for the old gladstone bags in which we carried wigs; the naturalist of old has become a sort of mythical and untrustworthy, even a slightly ludicrous and shameful, forebear of the entomologist, the dendrologist and their brothers. We divide and divide again and again, yet when we take stock of the division it may seem that the parts are not quite equal to the whole. Gilbert White or Mrs. Loudon could not be copied by a symposium of articles by subsidiary specialists, however learned each might be. And, in the matter of practical convenience, conversation would become well-nigh impossible and deadly dull if we were obliged to use each word with scientific exactitude. So, while one side of our nature makes us dissect the world with the finest scalpels, another draws us towards unity: we are prosaic and poetic by turns.

I soon found trouble with this conspiracy of opposites. My paper ration one day produced the last few pages of a book by Sir James Jeans on Planck's Constant, translated into French; and although physics had never reached such a level in my world, I was able after many days of concentration to understand the argument, which, I imagine, was set out for novices.

But what held my attention was a remark made by the author at the conclusion to the effect that Planck had shown a unit of ultimate atomicity to which no physical concept could be attached, that, in other words, the irreducibly smallest measurement in the physical world was not of a tiny particle nor of a tiny wave but of something rather weakly called an 'action', which had no physical form to offer to the mind's eye. He shaded this observation, which must have been somewhat perplexing for any professional measurer, by admitting that it was impossible to say how definite it would prove. We might, he suggested, have uncovered only a corner of the picture, and if more were visible we might see the problem very differently.

Although this was really a commonplace, such as must be made by every scientist sooner or later to justify further research, it occurred to me that it described knowledge. For we are always in one of two conditions; either we claim to know with assurance, in which case we are certain to have a successor who will make us seem ignorant; or, alternatively, we admit that what we know is imperfect.

The second condition is the more honest, and if we examine it more closely we may see that there is a rather even consistency in the ignorance we confess. Indeed, the nature of learning is like the digging of a mole. He enters the earth at the point of his choosing and he digs until he comes up at another point. If we had moles who dug right through the earth, they would still come up on the same surface. If the digging, therefore, is like our learning, the discovered surface is like knowledge; there always seems to be an unburrowed desert around the point of exit, but the available area is nevertheless limited.

There were many other interesting extensions of this simile: do we confuse mountains and molehills, mistaking our scrabblings of knowledge for the realities of nature and using the vagaries of nature as demonstrations of our knowledge? And is there perhaps an analogy between the pattern of these imaginary burrows and the nature of mathematics? But I let them pass. The conclusion which I was tempted to draw from it was that a part of our thought and language concerns the surface of knowledge, and it is likely that in due course it may cover the whole surface; but that there is another part which seems to concern the atmosphere and the universe beyond the surface and of which we can have no knowledge in this strict sense; and this is a part which remains constant in any age, irrespective of the number of holes that have been dug.

In this second part of our experience, our manner of communication is hampered by the fact that we use words which were, so to speak, coined underground, with the result that all our experience on this level has something of the status of a family joke; it can be alluded to but not properly described, and people outside the family do not understand at all. Happiness, I think, is in this class, and love, too, which was, I believe, defined by the Schoolmen as appetite modified by happiness.

Fear, on the other hand, seems less elusive. It is as though fear was a field of grass, with innumerable blades but always beneath us, accessible and palpable; while happiness and its kin are more like a hidden light which we know by the scattered stars which catch it but which we can only know by reflection, aware of the source but never seeing it.

Then, in the course of time, we allow some words to lose their primary significance and to acquire an allusive value on this upper plane, until, once they are well established there, we bring them down again. Love starts perhaps as some quite fleshly feeling, although cosmic in strength and in duration; it is sublimated by Plato and St. John and returns, *via* the *Roman de la Rose*, to Freudian sex and Hollywood. When a word has become so garbled in its direct significance it is difficult to use it even as an allusion. Meaning, as Swift said of reason, 'is a very light rider and easily shook off.'

Having leisure without end, I could spend as much time on this game of words as the energy of my brain allowed. If I was the yokel poaching on philosophers' preserves, that was no worry to me, there being more hole than fence around them; but I realized how sadly ill-equipped I was and often caught myself holding the most absurd internal dialogues and believing them of great importance.

If Auguste Comte, as I have heard say, wrote for forty years only to find that he had repeated Aristotle, I should confess to having spent more than once forty hours enthralled by some tautology which the *Concise Oxford Dictionary* would have exposed at a glance. I hankered after books, and still more after paper and pencil, so that I could dispense with the repetition of every argument that crossed my mind.

But I enjoyed the pastime and valued it, perhaps inordinately. For I viewed myself as a free man, waiting for the door to open on a new life. Where formerly each little wheel and wire which made up the machinery of life had seemed in turn to be the motor, fed by the fickle current of my consciousness, now the detachment of these months of solitude showed that none of them was of great power by itself and that all moved in an intricate movement which was but little disturbed by my absence or presence. Subjectively, I remained implicated in this movement, but objectively I had been removed from the centre to the rim. And it was because the rim of the driven wheel is most affected by the driving that I applied myself with considerable diligence to its study and to the bringing forth, like Toletanes in the Frankeleyn's Tale, of my tables

Ful wel corrected...
As been his centres, and his arguments,
And his proporcionels convenients
For his equacions in every thing.

If it was no more, it was an exercise which prevented atrophy. But I must confess that it kindled no love in me for the Toad, nor for later and more vicious enemies.

卌 卌

Chapter 11

Spring had done its work, and the square of sky in my window was deepening with the full warmth of summer. I shivered, ridiculously draped in blankets, while Paris was full of cotton frocks and new blood tingled through bodies lazily stretching in the sun. But my slow body was lagging behind the seasons: although I knew that Easter was past I dismissed my old impatience from my mind, seeing such promise in the summer weather that no reservation, with its hidden pessimism, was now necessary.

From my blind eyrie I could see France in panorama, field upon field peopled with pickers and harvesters, with figures busy at spraying the vines and scything the hay, while symbolic bees buzzed in the remaining space. Villages on hilltops and towns by riversides had emptied their belongings out into the streets again and ant-like crowds of women bustled round them.

And at night, in the warm south wind on lonely heaths and pastures, quick silent groups were welcoming friends from England and storing the cases of guns and gelignite with which, one

127

day soon, they would noisily send the Germans on their way. England I could not see, but I could guess, even be sure, that they had the troops and the equipment for a landing. Now they would be planning the time. If they did not come in June they would spare the harvest and wait until September—the first week in September, so that the landings would be done before the gales came. I could be patient for three more months.

The prospect was marred only by the thought, which came to me sometimes when I considered the end, that I would have done nothing towards it. All my dreams had been futile. They had burned themselves out and had not resulted in even the useful movement of my little finger. Had I done harm? I scoured my memory of the last interrogation for anything I had let fall, but was never sure one way or the other, only doubting the worst.

Then, one morning, the muscle-brained corporal clattered into my cell and sharply ordered me to collect all my possessions and follow him. I had become unused to the dangerous side of life. Footsteps no longer stopped me in my tracks until they passed, and it was but rarely that I woke in the morning with the sense of doom, a sort of self-abdication, which I had made my daily oracle, like Cassandra at Argos, in the early months. Now I was suddenly jolted back. My stomach turned over abruptly, and I cursed my illusion and my disappointment and tried to imagine what was going to happen, conjuring up pictures of the rue des Saussaies and the worse places at which I guessed.

I was put at ease again before my mind had begun to clear, for the corporal took me along the floor to cell No. 259 and locked me in again without a word, leaving me to wonder for a while whether I could settle down here or whether this was the first movement of a series which would lead much farther. It was characteristic of the apathy of these men that they never thought to put us out of our misery of anticipation, although the slightest effort of imagination must have suggested it to them. They were content to bark '*Komm!*' and to strut grimly behind until the mission was accomplished, with never another word, unless it was '*Los!*', which was a nervous tic on all their tongues.

It did not take me long to recover my balance, swearing that I would never again let myself sink into such complacency (but swearing, of course, in vain). And when I had decided that I had simply changed cells again I found that the new one, even in the light of a fine morning, compared unfavourably with the worst of its predecessors. It was slovenly without being filthy; the cement round the toilet had crumbled and gave the impression of a dank and mouldering outhouse; one pane of the skylight was missing, and a draught blew steadily through it; finally, the blankets were torn and threadbare and the straw-sack strawless. But I had by now a more dispassionate view of discomfort, and when I considered the fineness of the day, my good fortune in still being in the prison and the fact that it was nearly midday, I was able to overlook all these changes for the worse. The blankets would not be so important in summer, and the missing window-pane even appeared as a blessing when I saw how much more immediate was my contact with the outside world and felt the warmth and fragrance of the fresh air which eddied through it. If I climbed onto the table I could see the red tiles of the building opposite, and this gave me a strange feeling that I had regained my foot-hold on earth, like seeing the light suddenly at the far end of a tunnel.

Soon after this my birthday came, and because I had been lucky in having birthdays properly remembered by my family and friends, I woke with a silly feeling in the back of my mind that it would be a most suitable day for a surprise.

I dismissed the idea quickly enough and passed the morning in moderate contentment thinking of birthdays past and particularly of birthday cake. It was a Wednesday, and the Germans were now treating Wednesdays as Saturdays, sending the staff on leave for the afternoon and abandoning us to that deserted silence which made the day seem twice as long and our state more derelict than ever because these were the only times when none of the dreamed-of strokes of fortune could be delivered for lack of sergeants. When I heard them thrusting their keys into the locks before leaving, it was with a habitual relapse into depression and the fancy that it would, after all, have been comforting if I had had a second helping of soup. I would have felt fuller, on the one hand, and, on the other, my sense of individuality would have been bolstered, however implausibly. But my discipline was strong now, and I was soon back to pacing the floor and telling myself beautiful stories of the life outside. Once or twice I teased myself with the suggestion that some little token now, when ordinary hope was passed, would serve to reaffirm my knowledge that I was not lost and helpless. But I brushed it off quickly, knowing its frivolity.

The last shaft of sunlight left my wall, and the deepening of the sky told me that the day was nearly over. I would tell myself one more story, I said, and then I would have my *moment musical*, and it would be supper-time. But the door burst suddenly open, and a little red-headed sergeant scampered in in canvas shoes. Before I could make myself aware of his arrival, he had snatched the lid off a large biscuit-box which he was carrying under one arm and had emptied the contents onto my bed. Then he instantly disappeared, and I heard his rubber-shod footsteps padding down the passage.

The *deus* having safely delivered himself of his message and returned to the shelter of the *machina*, the chorus started its many-voiced comment. Alarm, belated, was followed by confusion, bewilderment, joy and embarrassment. For my blanket was covered with biscuits and their debris.

Here was clearly no normal event. In retrospect I can imagine many reasons for which the *feldwebel* might rationally have given me some chocolate, but even today there is no apparent justification for the appearance of a red-headed sergeant.

No other doors were opened in my hearing; it was later than the hours of duty even on an ordinary day. It was just possible that the staff kept a list of prisoners who received no parcels and made special distributions of this kind from time to time. But once in ten months? And one at a time, at this hour of the evening? As a mystery, it piqued me; but as a happening it rather confused me. For I was no longer compelled to justify everything which happened by elaborating a clear and positive chain of causes leading to it.

I was quite content to accept that whatever came, came from God's wish that it should be so, and I had only a passing interest in the intermediate steps. I had no knowledge of this, in the sense that I knew what would happen if I pressed the tap, nor was it belief, in the sense that I believed myself to have been born on a certain date. It was rather a state or condition, into which I had passed unwittingly and for no apparent reason except perhaps that the equilibrium of solitude would bring anyone near it who was not crippled with some spiritual rheumatism.

But if I was sure of the authority of Providence, I had few expectations of providential generosity, feeling that in most things normality must run its course and that if I went free from prison I would be able to count that a mercy big enough to last one lifetime. And it was for this reason that I was inclined to subdue the almost irrepressible temptation to, as it were, drop hints that this or that small favour would cost little and help much. Such petty things seemed out of proportion, even impudent. Therefore I was embarrassed when I remembered that I had been dallying with idle thoughts of just this kind today.

Meanwhile my gluttony, uninhibited by wonder or the hesitations of the flimsier reaches of the mind, had me counting my blessings with meticulous avarice. I laid the biscuits on the shelf in piles of half a dozen and found in the end that there were precisely ninety-six, with the equivalent of another dozen in fragments and crumbs which I left on the blanket.

Then, with the same fastidious prudence which had always proved a sham in the past but was still called for by some conservative bogey, I calculated how to ration them. A dozen a day for eight days or two dozen a day for four? I crammed my mouth full of broken pieces from the blanket and decided to be bold. I would not ration them; if I could eat them all today, I would. They would be a birthday treat and nothing more.

As it turned out, they lasted six days, because I over-ate with abandon that first evening and my dysentery came back and left me unable to do more than nibble. One of my back teeth also gave way towards the end, and then another, so that until the end of the war I was obliged to eat like a rabbit with the front pairs.

I reflected, when the shelf was bare, that my appetite was as tiresome when it was satisfied as when it was starved, but this did not prevent me wishing for a more constant supply, nor did the slight sourness of the reflection damp my happiness with what had happened. I only wondered whether Providence should not have balanced the diet more judiciously. So much dry food, I doubted, could not be good without some fat.

For a while nothing happened to interrupt my mild contentment. Each morning I woke knowing that today would not bring the good news, but that it was coming. I found a new pleasure in my absurd routine. The manicure made me think of leisurely comfort; the exercises (now less ambitious) of free exercise; and my catechism of general knowledge took me roaming through the world, a world much more beautiful than the one I knew.

Afterwards, I thought of the clothes I would have to buy; my taste had become rugged, and I thought only of the heaviest tweeds and the thickest brogues; and the unpaid bills which had assumed unaccustomed weight upon my conscience when I had thought I would never be in a position to pay them, now became a pleasant duty to look forward to.

The summer shimmered gently on. As my patch of sky became

misted with the heat there arose a new loudness in the air. Each day more and more aircraft came over, and the alarms, which sent the prison staff securing all the locks and taking refuge downstairs, grew longer and longer, until, on the Fourteenth of July, there was what seemed to be a victory parade. Squadron after squadron flew across, and the whole prison was afire with excitement. I could hear the others singing the *Marseillaise* all day long, and I became infected and sang too.

After this day the parades became regular, and I was certain that they were the heralds, if not the companions, of invasion. With one toe on the window-skirting and one hand gripping the flimsy skylight, I climbed up until I could see the whole sky in front of me and, if I screwed my head round as far as it would go, some trees.

From there I saw the formations passing over. I was not sure how many aircraft there should be in each but I assumed them to be in multiples of eleven and anxiously counted to make sure that none was missing. And I made vast and carefree computations of the havoc they were wreaking and pictured regiments in hot pursuit across the ruins of enemy divisions.

Little did I guess that when the day came, a year later, the ruins would be those of Caen and the dead in them more French than German.

It was clear that the raids and our most transparent joy at them were making the guards sensitive and surly. One Wednesday a *feldwebel* came round and said that there was to be no singing during raids and that no one was allowed to look out of the window.

Soon after that I was hanging at my precarious watch-post looking out into the reddening sky over Ivry. A raid was just ending, and the anti-aircraft guns were falling into a cautious diminuendo, when there was a sudden vivid flash, like a magnesium flare, just above the sun. For a moment I did not realize what had happened; then I saw black smoke and something falling, and knew that a plane had been hit. Sickly, I watched it flutter, then break in two and flash with a quick pale flame against the sun as it dropped behind the trees. All England seemed in agony before my eyes.

I had not heard the footstep outside the door, nor the cover of the peep-hole sliding up. The door crashed open while I was still staring through the trees, and the Toad stamped in. I felt a great wish to wring his neck at that moment, and he probably perceived both my thought and its futility, for he cursed me profusely and at length with a potpourri of gutturals, sibilants and pure explosives; but he did not touch me, and after a stirring peroration he went out.

I guessed that I had not heard the last of him, and a few minutes later the bat-eared corporal came in. He said nothing, perhaps realizing that his master had spoiled the audience, but laconically hauled my mattress out of the cell. Then he came back, searched the cell, found nothing and left me.

The penalty moved me not at all, unless it were to flippancy. The floor was scarcely less hospitable than the bed, and I lay down that night with the same appreciation of rude comfort in a righteous cause which is normally the privilege of those who sleep rarely in camp beds. In the morning I woke, having slept deeply, and felt that the goodness of life was unimpaired. But at midday the soup clattered past my door without stopping. For a moment I thought it had been absent-minded and was about to hammer on the door to call it back, but it soon became clear to me that this was a part of the punishment which had, by the nature of things, been delayed.

I must confess that it was a bleak moment. But the hardest blow was the thought that if I had no soup, I would not only have to fill in the twenty minutes or so which, with delicate spooning, I could spend eating it, but I would also have to be patient for twice as long: the days would be doubled. The soup itself, I assured myself, was of no nutritional value whatsoever, and I need not fear starvation, especially in summer. It was a mere insulator which separated the walls of my stomach for a short while. But I was not happy on the first day. I kept my temper and my bread, but in the afternoon I decided to go mad until something happened to restore the situation. I tried to remember pieces from Shake-speare and shouted them to my four walls at the top of my voice. But nobody paid any attention. Perhaps they were too used to madmen to be bothered with them. And I found, after I had anticked for a while, that madness was no more to be had for the wishing now than it had been earlier.

On the second day, and the third and the fourth, I experienced no more than a mild disgruntlement when I woke to think of a soupless day, and the pang caused by the passing trolley was short if sharp. The weather was still fine and the planes were still passing over. I even climbed back to my perch to watch them. But on the fourth day the soup stopped at my door once more, and soon after it the corporal silently dragged in my mattress.

Ḥ Ḥ I

Chapter 12

My door opened rather quietly one day, and I looked up to see the padre standing on the threshold. He was holding the Bible in one hand, stretched out towards me, and when I hesitated, he said: 'Would this be of any use to you?'

I was unable to respond to any interruption of my meditations without a space to readjust my senses, and I was neither quite sure what he was offering me nor certain of my attitude to him. In my confusion, therefore, I invited him in. But he shook his head and offered me the book again so brusquely that I took it; and we exchanged no further word. He closed the door again, and in a moment the sergeant came to lock it.

The fact penetrated my mind that not only had I now enough reading to occupy me for some months but also the whole text from which so many excerpts had been stumbling-blocks to me was now open to inspection.

During the next months, the rest of my time in Fresnes, I read the entire volume more than two times through, with the exception of Leviticus, Numbers and Deuteronomy, at which I looked only infrequently and with trepidation. It was in a French translation, and although the language lacked the magnificence of the King James version, I found it in some ways easier to read, if only because the tags were in new clothes and offered themselves for inspection instead of mere recognition. A good part of the Jacobean phraseology has been so drummed into childish heads already amply encumbered by the current language of necessity that it has become almost parenthetical to many of us and meant, at least to me, as little as a soldier's oaths. Some of it seen in an unfamiliar form loses its sterility: *'Je vous dis...'* is less ornamental but more plainly direct than 'I say unto you...'

Nevertheless, I was never able to conceive the Bible as a whole book. The Psalms and the Gospels seemed to be coherent, since both represented (with a few psalms excepted) an assertion of the delight in being a creature of a God who delighted in your being His creature.

The high hills are a refuge for the wild goats;
and the rocks for the conies.

This was something I had seen and could understand.

Are not five sparrows sold for two farthings,
and not one of them is forgotten before God?

This also was of a familiar certainty to me.

But I had at the same time to abstain from any veneration of the historical and prophetic Old Testament, which, although it was an unsurpassable literary blessing to me, never became more than history; and even in my early schooldays I had preferred Thucydides and Herodotus. Now the absence of the language which had set it apart from all the others made it seem barely distinguished, and I even doubted whether it was fitted to be incorporated with the Gospel.

> *'And ye shall be an execration, and an astonishment, and a curse, and a reproach....'*

St. Paul, too, seemed to be making more of the words of Jesus than there was in them. Perhaps the parts of his epistles which offended me were directed specially to the Jews in the special language of their tradition, as had been some of the sayings of Jesus. But for the ordinary person it seemed that the menace

> *'In flaming fire taking vengeance on them that know not God'*

was less patient than the shepherd who went into the mountains to seek the hundredth sheep. The primitive idea of sacrifice seemed also to interpenetrate his letters too persistently.

And who ordained that the Book of Revelation should be annexed to the Christian texts? Why not rather Bunyan, or even Blake? The inclusion of the Book of Joshua, for example, seemed to me to be understandable if the Bible had been compiled as a Testament by somebody who believed that history was necessary evidence for belief in the irrational. But how was this curious symbolism to be construed either as evidence or as an extension of the subject of belief?

> *These are the two olive trees, and the two candlesticks standing before the God of the earth, and if any man will hurt them, fire pro-ceedeth out of their mouth, and devoureth their enemies: and if any man will hurt them, he must in this manner be killed.*

This (lest I should commit the error of offence to anybody—and I myself might be wiser after the event) was the impression which I received from a reading of the Bible which was informed, perhaps with a spirit of criticism and perhaps under the cloud of some resentment at the evasiveness of my early reminiscences, but certainly by a desire hearing to understand and seeing to perceive; and by a certainty, moreover, that what made streams run to the sea would not leave me to eddy uselessly round a cliff of words.

And then, one day, when the corporal had passed with the paper, he came back unexpectedly after supplying the next cell and handed me a bundle wrapped in a large handkerchief. I asked him what it was, but he just said '*Kamerad*' and left me. I untied the handkerchief and found inside a great assortment of food: hard-boiled eggs, chestnut preserve, nuts, an apple and sweet biscuits. It was a feast beyond all my dreams, and I gazed at it in awe for several minutes. Then I realized that it was the prisoner in No. 260 who had sent it to me, although I did not understand the complacency of the corporal. I went to the wall and started tapping, but I heard a remote voice saying:

'Come and talk through the tap.'

The plumbing was so arranged that there was a hollow between the adjoining corners of our cells, containing the pipes for our taps and toilets, and by speaking through the hole which housed the taps we could communicate fairly clearly.

I started to say the best thanks I could express, but my neighbour would hear none of them.

'That's nothing,' he said. 'I'll send you some more soon, as soon as I get another parcel.'

I asked him how he received parcels, not without offering myself the illusion that I might be able to make some arrangement for myself.

'My wife brings me one almost every week,' he replied; 'but why don't you get any?'

I explained that I was English, since this was now no secret but rather a source of unearned pride; and we exchanged names.

He called himself Bernard, his real name, as I now know, being Edmond Michelet, who was later Minister of War. He gave me the latest news from the Mediterranean, which I found disappointing, and then asked me why I did not join in the evening conversations through the windows.

I did not like to admit that the real reason was that I was so used to silence and so privately engaged in my own thoughts that I found conversation an embarrassment, so I said that it was too difficult to climb up to the skylight, which was flimsy and might collapse with disastrous results. (My earlier experience with this occurred to me also, but I could not mention it.) Bernard thought little of this obstacle, being a truly French believer in the virtue of conversation, and explained that if I could not open the window I could probably loosen one of the panes in such a way that it could be removed and replaced at will. And I suddenly felt, in the face of this desire for my company, that it would be good, after all, to be able to talk, and I examined my window carefully to see what could be done.

The lock was firm and would not yield, but one of the panes seemed to have been scratched almost free of putty. It was held in place by four small nails bent through 270 degrees, and by turning these the pane would undoubtedly come out. It was easy to turn the nails, but the glass fitted against the outside of the frame, and if it were freed it would fall outward on to the sill and break. But investigation produced its wonted obstinacy, and I found a piece of wire which had been wrapped round one leg of my stool for no apparent reason and, breaking it in two pieces, devised a system of grapples with which I could lower the pane forward and return it to its place with some safety.

Meanwhile, Bernard had told the cells above us about me, and when I was at last ready to talk I found a small club waiting for me. Both of the upper cells had three or four inhabitants, but each was represented by a single spokesman, that above Bernard by André and that above me by Michel, who had a deep

141

and powerful voice with which he bellowed the daily 'news' and sang raucous songs at night.

Although the friendliness of these people made me glad, I was not at my ease with them. I found conversation one-sided, because I had little small talk, and discursiveness was not encouraged by our method of shouting through the window. So my part was mostly said in monosyllables. And between none of us was there any but the most trivial talk.

The dramatic law might have required an exchange of noble thoughts among men who neither knew nor could see each other; but such thoughts as we had were too deeply conceived to be easily prised loose or too peculiar to our privacy to be lightly thrown into the public place. For we had all spent our hours of meditation. So I could see only fleetingly into the characters of my companions. Of Michel I only knew that he was cheerful and noisy, of André that he was quiet. Bernard, too, was quiet, but with a potent tranquillity which enabled him to give encouragement that did not seem mere brave words. He had anxieties, for he was married and had numerous children, but he seemed quite free of inner perplexities, making me resent my own.

I saw Bernard once when we went out for our rare exercise. He was older than I had imagined, though it was hard to guess age from a face hidden in dark stubble. He was quite unabashed at taking up our friendship face to face, waiting for me at the corner of the stairs as if we had been on the platform at Victoria Station, in London, and saying something casual about his next parcel as one might arrange a next meeting while catching a train. For my part, I found it by no means so easy to be casual and would have needed much longer before saying anything intelligible. But our shepherds brooked no dawdling, and the moment was gone before I could construe my disordered thoughts into a sentence.

Bernard was not alone in coming to my rescue. His first contribution came on a Tuesday, and I spent the whole day eating until at last I felt really full and as happy as I could imagine possible. A more temperate man, I thought again, would have shown more prudence and restraint, but I had enough prudence on ordinary days and decided that anything over the ration should be eaten as my appetite dictated and not put in the dismal company of my bread. I was happy for a few days; then, on Friday, when I am afraid I was beginning to look forward to Bernard's next parcel (a greed which I always repented but could never quite suppress), Michel called down to me at sunset.

'*Hé, Christophe!*'

I called back that I was listening.

'This evening,' he shouted, 'when it's dark, you'll hear me thump on the floor. Go to your window and we'll let down some food.'

Some organ near my heart rebounded with pleasure and anticipation, but I was immediately sobered when I remembered that I could not reach to the bars at the far edge of the outer windowsill and would never be able to retrieve anything which hung beyond them. I called back to Michel that I was grateful for his thoughtfulness but explained why I could not be its beneficiary.

'Look at your bed,' was his reply, made with the calm certainty of a seer, 'and you will find that one of the cross-pieces is loose. It will be long enough to reach. But mind you come to the window as soon as you hear my signal.'

I looked under the mattress, and the second of the iron slats proved to be loose. It was also hooked at one end. Whether it was an accepted trick of the prison which Michel, with his superior resourcefulness, had already found out, or whether he was guessing and relying on my ingenuity to loosen a bar if he was wrong, I never knew. Certainly it was the ideal tool for the purpose.

About an hour after dark, the most terrifying crashes broke out over my head. All four of the denizens of the cell must have taken part, and I was a little doubtful whether so much advertisement would not bring sentries running from far and wide to frustrate our plan. But it would have been impossible to trace the sound in that building except from very close at hand, and we had a warning system of knocks which gave warning of a sentry on his rounds. This did not provide complete safety on our floor, because a sentry might double back, and a single man would not always notice him. But nobody disturbed us this time.

I opened my loose pane and at once saw a bulky handkerchief slowly drop to the level of the sill. I shouted that it was down and hooked the string with my iron bar, hauling the packet in, emptying it and then giving the signal to haul it up again. The whole operation lasted a few seconds, and as I put my pane back into place I shouted my thanks.

'*Bon appétit!*' came the reply.

Some days later, Michel called down again and said he would repeat the performance that evening. It would be better this time, he said, and recited a long list of eggs, marmalade, biscuits, chocolate and I forget what else. I was inclined for a moment to make a conventional protest and to tell him not to send me more, but it seemed on reflection to be neither sincere nor friendly, so I contented myself with thanks which were halting but genuine. Spoiling by these unseen brethren had refurbished my appetite with a fancy for sweets and rich things which it had long forgotten, and I spent the rest of the day looking forward to a night of gluttony.

This time, however, all was not well. The thumping brought me to my window, hook in hand, water in mouth, and I peered up for the descending bundle. It came jerkily into sight, and Michel called to ask if it was low enough.

'Another metre and a half,' I told him.

There was another jerk, and then the bundle suddenly felt like a plummet past me and out of sight.

'Have you got it?' asked Michel.

'No,' I said, though I could hardly speak. 'It's fallen.'

Michel swore, and we all shut our windows quickly; and I

went to sleep after I had worn myself out with fury and with eating chocolate in my imagination.

Early the next morning, the Toad marched in with his two corporals and a young and pleasant-looking *feldwebel* who was plainly one of the senior prison staff. The corporals went to the window and tried the lock, while the *feldwebel* asked me outright whether anybody had tried to pass me a package. He was so forthright and candid in manner that I was for a moment tempted to treat him likewise. It would have been a relief after so many months of caution and deceit. But I was not the principal in the affair, so I simply answered 'No', with not too much surprise nor yet too little.

'So,' he said, looking at me with the same directness and with no trace of malignity. 'Perhaps I should ask the people above you whether they tried.' And he added inconsequentially: 'They have enough for themselves.'

I said that it would not be of much use to me unless he were to open my window, and he laughed loudly without saying anything further. He went to the window and looked round it, while my pulse quickened, and then he clicked his tongue, glanced at me with a kind of quizzical satisfaction and said:

'I'm afraid the dog got it.'

Then they all left, and I heard no more of the episode, but I was quick to relay the gist of it up to Michel, who escaped as lightly. There was, after all, a German with a sense of proportion.

After this, André took a hand in my nourishment. It was more difficult, because he had to swing across to me on a long line; and I was by now becoming embarrassed, because I wondered whether I was not becoming something of a beggar. But the whole episode was soon closed. One night I fumbled. The pane of glass pivoted round the nail which held one edge, my hook slipped on the other edge, and nothing was left but smithereens.

The Toad saw the damage in the morning, and there was a noisy scene in which my role was silent but not unruffled. The bat-eared corporal was sent for and with hammer, nails and muscle matched his master's verbal pleonasms and made sure that the window which had never been opened in the past would remain closed in the future. Then a prisoner was brought under guard to replace the broken pane. I watched him carefully, to see where he placed the nails, for the putty was easy to cut through with my piece of wire, but I knew at the same time that the scope of that ruse had been exhausted, and any lingering ambition to renew it was finally quashed when I was again deprived of soup for three days.

꜀꜀꜀꜀꜀ ꜀꜀꜀꜀꜀ ||

Chapter 13

Meanwhile Bernard left us. The Germans hauled in their nets in August and were filling the prisons with a mixed catch of maquisards,[1] innocent bystanders and petty felons. But the prisons were full, so the earlier victims and the condemned were sent to Germany to make room. There was a great coming and going in Fresnes, and every day we heard the sounds of departing exiles.

The window-shouters had let us know of their omniscience what was astir, but I saw no portent in it until Bernard left. He was called with almost no warning to collect his things and go below. It was said (and rightly, in the event) that the convoy was bound for Saarbrücken, nominally a transit camp, but one of the worst in the whole system and a grave for many. When he told us of what had happened the air outside our little group of windows became suddenly still with horror, as if we were for the first time aware that we were not the audience but the players of a tragedy

---

1   Members of the Maquis, rural bands of fighters supporting the Resistance.

and that our friend was no mere voice in the chorus but the first target of the Furies to be swallowed up. We bade him good-bye with hollow words, and he went cheerfully.

Bernard's cell was occupied again within the hour, but the days of my emergence were almost past, and I retreated once more into true solitude, only rarely broken. The threat, now declared, of being sent to Germany made me cherish my isolation so much that reluctance to go back into a world of change and movement, of collision and interruption, grew stronger than simple exasperation at the prospect of moving away from liberty, which seemed a natural course for my perverse destiny to choose.

Experience had shown me the irony with which fate treats would-be rivals, and if ever I allowed the thought of going to Germany to depress me to the point of revolt, I had a vision of the liberation of France, in which everything would be freed but the prisoners, who had dreamed of it through the hours month after month, and who were lost among the endless forests and hills of Germany. It seemed as perversely appropriate and inevitable as the marriage of Oedipus, and was beyond argument or protest. But the movement, the mingling, the doing of things ordered, the replying to questions asked, the need to notice, listen, talk, comply, accommodate, reveal, conceal, the effort of reaction and volition for the sake of mere survival—the return, in short, to reality and society, but in their worst aspects, made me shrink into my cell as if I would lose myself there.

For a little while yet there was hope that it would not happen. The air raids continued, and there was a hubbub and a tension in the prison all day long which held the promise of great things impending. But nothing happened, and soon September was gone; and I knew that there was the whole winter in which to reach my turn for deportation. But this cloud, like the others, quickly retired below the horizon and only reappeared at intervals, as if to prevent or punish an excess of complacency.

At the same time, I had a more practical preoccupation with the coming winter, which would find me at a yet greater disadvantage than the previous year. The process of physical degeneration had taken a strange turn, as if to *reculer pour mieux sauter*,[2] since, although my neck and arms remained as scraggy as those of a plucked fowl, my legs were beginning to swell sluggishly from the feet upward. I only noticed them after the blight was well advanced, and when I saw two great fat white knees, like that 'woman whom nobody loves', I thought with dismay that I might just as well become a monk if they were to remain thus, since the most loving eyes could not but be repelled by them.

Less disgusting but more disturbing was the realization that the shivering which I had noticed as abnormal in the spring had continued throughout the summer, even on the warmest days. When I considered this I wondered whether the winter would not at least bring on pneumonia. Knowing nothing of physiology or medicine, I considered the problem for a while in a scientific spirit, but a fortunate accident turned my ingenuity to more fruitful ends before I perceived that I was wasting it.

Of my two blankets one was brown and the other grey, the former a veritable rag, the latter thicker and still large enough to wrap round me. It so happened that while I was considering a formula for combining their two warmths into the most efficient whole, I noticed a small sliver of glass lying on the window-frame. It was no doubt a relic of my summer freedom and had escaped notice in the dust. It had a sharp edge, and I had no sooner picked it up than I realized that I had all the elements of the tailor's trade ready to my hand. The glass would serve as shears, my little pieces of wire, unused since I mishandled them on the window, would bend into serviceable needles, and the blankets would provide both cloth and thread. It struck me at the same time that the

2   French: to step back to make a better jump.

smaller blanket would be more useful if it were converted into some shape which would lie closely round me, and I conceived the idea of making a waistcoat of it.

I did not know at the time that the penalty for work of this kind, called sabotage, was death, but I recognized that the mutilation of prison stores, however dilapidated, would scarcely be approved, and I therefore decided that the design of the waistcoat must be such that the blanket would retain its roughly rectangular shape after the necessary cutting, so that elegant curves and wasted snippets would not attract attention. The pattern was thus of the simplest contrivance. Three strips girded the chest, and two supported them over the shoulders; sewn together with thread from the same blanket, they composed what I considered to be a garment.

I spent a few weeks making it, sitting on the bed facing the door and working behind my raised knees, so that my industry could not be seen from the peep-hole; and when it was finished in elementary form I added buttons, a collar and patch-pockets and then disguised its primitive design by the deceitful embroidering of false seams in thread from the grey blanket. As may be clear from this description, I was proud of my product, but I none the less wore it under my shirt. Not only was concealment wise, but when I shivered I wriggled and the rubbing of the rough wool on my skin gave me the tactile illusion of warmth. It was a source of warmth and comfort to me until 1945, when a young Russian so flattered my craftsman's pride with his unbounded admiration that I gave it to him.

Sewing, if Dr. Johnson had but known it, concentrates the mind even more wonderfully than an anticipated execution, which, for my part, had rather distracted it. As a moribund, I was like a ship tossing between Scylla and Charybdis; as a tailor, like a small canoe paddling from Hong Kong to Valparaiso.

When I became a working man again and literate, I reordered my routine, keeping the morning manicure and mental work-out for sentimental reasons, because I was used to them, but abandoning all but the lightest of physical exercises. I walked much less, too, and instead spent most of the morning reading my Bible and the light hours of the afternoon sewing. Then for two or three hours in the evening I had the choice between walking up and down or sitting and trying to solve whatever problem had occurred to me.

On reading the Bible, I had been persuaded that it contained certain internal contradictions which could be summed up as the conflict between Wrath and Love. Since the far-off Sunday when I had first recalled the fatted calf I had been almost unconsciously staking my reason—and at least my hope—to the authority of the parable, but in face of so many contradictions it seemed unreasonable to do so. God could not be Shepherd and Scourge at once, and the wrathful God of the Bible was not a Shepherd coaxing stray sheep with His crook, but a bad-tempered and sometimes unfeeling one belabouring His flock as it were without cause. The acerbity of His temper was even reflected in some passages of the Gospels. I noticed, too, in this newly critical mood, that events seemed to tally as well with this dual account as with any other; more than one setback had driven me to the verge of renouncing hope. But hope had in the meanwhile been displaced by firm conviction, inarticulate and incoherent but unyielding; and the seemingly insoluble antagonism between belief and reason threatened to explode in insanity.

But again insanity failed to keep its promise of accommodation, and I solved the whole problem by realizing simply that I had not understood what I was reading, or rather that I had only understood a part. My earlier theory of allusions, of family jokes, seemed to fit the reading of scripture as well as the understanding of abstract nouns. For if scripture was concerned with the relationship of man to God, it was dealing with the irrational, and communication between one man and another about the irrational is a matter of allusion and, yet more, of chance. What was then more likely than that a single man's appreciation of a vast composition like the Bible would depend, as it were, on the kind of family he belonged to and, therefore, the kind of joke he understood? I found that I responded to some, but not all, of the Christian allusions, while the menaces and the pessimism and the obscure passages struck no chord in me. With that I was passably content. The problem had become as one of taste: not to be disputed.

I was worried, too, by the old notions of 'evil' and 'sin', which had been so integral a part of what I had been taught about religion. It was not enough to dislike them; they were so firmly accepted and (or because) so constantly repeated that they had also to be disposed of on grounds which I could conscientiously admit. I had understood evil, perhaps because of my idleness, to be as it were an element, and an absolute at that, but it was now clear to me that if, as I believed, the only absolute was God, and good by definition, there could be no such *thing* as evil: all it could be was an epithet meaning 'less than Good'.

Perhaps that is all it ever has meant in the scholarly world, but in my ordinary little world there had been built around the 'principle of evil' a whole ethic which could not be other than misleading, a polar system of values which began, perhaps, simply as an everyday simplification but which had grown into a fixed and general theory. An adjective, by being for centuries attached to every variety of imperfection, had been insidiously promoted to rank above Creation. And with what result? Fear, inhibition, moral despair and, above all, such preoccupation with the negative that men had no energy left with which to look positively after what was good. The Devil is only a dark glass.

I wished to replace this old polar system of value—the good of every kind faced with its evil opposite—by a scale which would all be positive degrees of good. The polar system seemed like a balance, with two different weights, used to demonstrate gravity.

Our demonstrators said: Gravity is all on the side of the heavier and against the lighter; but I would rather have it that Gravity works upon the entire system, and particularly on the pivot of the balance. There is no critical mark to the right of which is Good and to the left Evil. Life is not a gloomy and impossible grey, as moralists would have it, to be sorted into black and white: all its aspects form a spectrum, of which the greater part is hidden to a single pair of eyes, but which all originates from a single source. To suppose that there are contrary principles of light and darkness, or good and evil, is as presumptuous as to deny the existence of infrared light on the grounds of its invisibility.

Such a change in the scale of values does not entail much revision of the grosser forms of judgment. Things and actions will still be good or bad. But it does accompany a change of attitude: pessimism becomes optimism, and the good of life is no longer overshadowed by its imperfections. Henceforth, the tiniest window bringing light will always dominate the bleak and oppressive walls and the dangerous passages beyond them. And we will fight for what we love instead of pursuing what we hate.

Sin was the active and human form of this old evil, and it appeared to be an act of the will. Men are represented as coming to a forked road and, before they reach the cleft, performing some act which is quite independent of any mechanistic choice imposed by circumstances or contingency. This act, as I remembered it, was called the exercise of free will, and according to the direction it imposed the man sinned or was good.

But I both disliked this theory, on the grounds of its conformity with the principles of opposite good and evil, and doubted it on the grounds of logic. For this notion of free will seemed to be a premise stated *a priori*, from which the nature of sin was deduced as required; the whole theory rested upon an arbitrary assumption that human choice is a metaphysical cause of human action, or, if not metaphysical in the strict sense, then at least independent of any other factor that affected the person. But is such an assumption either obvious or necessary? Do we have any knowledge that makes it likely? Day after day I had faced a simple choice: would I or would I not eat my bread before the appointed time? Each day the balance was tilted this way and that by a mêlée of pros and cons. I want to eat because my stomach is empty and is sending urgent signals to my brain; I don't want to eat because my memory is sending equally urgent warnings of hungry and sleepless nights; early training bids me be strong in virtue, and experience bids me be strong in prudence. Sometimes one side gains the advantage, sometimes the other. Does eternity balance on such frivolities?

Every choice is offered by some fortuitous occasion, which sets in motion a battery of reflexes built up involuntarily (in respect of any given occasion); and it seems unnecessary to elevate a process, which can so readily be conceived as rational and mechanical, to the status of a cardinal metaphysical function.

If, however, the alliance of sin and free will is undone, some substitute must be found. For the idea of life as a purely mechanical process appears intuitively as fantastic and, in the realm of reason, is rebutted by the very existence of so universal a notion as that of responsibility. And it was this word and the French term for 'free will'—*libre arbitre*—which suggested that everything I had learned concerning the human act had suffered an immense distortion from a small but fundamental misconception: it was held that the quality of an act was determined by an act of volition which supposedly preceded it, whereas I now believed that consciousness of the value of any action was essentially reflective and could only be made crudely to precede the action by a process of forward imagination, in its turn an act of reflection.

At this small discovery all the paradoxes of the freedom of human beings over against the omnipotence of God dissolved. The paradox, as I thought it, of free will in an ordained creation was no longer necessary for the justification of the idea of merit;

that which supposed the influence of a principle opposite to God disappeared.

This anxious dilapidation of the old remembered traditions, until only the cornerstone remained, had to be followed by some new construction. Only a mystic can be satisfied by the bare immaterial summit of the arch; ordinary rational men, even the most distracted, require a coherent edifice reaching up from the ground of everyday experience. I was not equipped to undertake such a work of building, but I tried to visualize the outlines of the problem.

I believed that many of the problems of concept could be solved by supposing an analogy of the relationship between the facts and the laws of physical science. Laws describe an abstract order, but the facts, although they follow the laws, are always less precise than them. The level of experience seems always to be separated from the level of abstract order by some coarseness of actuality. In a similar way, we inhabit the outskirts of beauty, seeing its aspects, but always at a distance, or, as it were, through a haze, and never entering quite into the heart of it. And if abstract order and beauty can be perceived in the world of things, why should they not underlie the world of men?

I used to imagine that the soul of a man was like a little whiff of invisible gas, which was supposed to be released when he died. So I could not say that I believed in the soul. I now proposed to myself that every man was doubled by an abstract expression of himself, on the analogy of a physical occurrence being doubled by a mathematical expres-sion. But I named this abstract self 'genius', probably in order to avoid the associations of the word 'soul'. It would have form of its own kind and balance with its surroundings, and the two halves of the diptych would be separated by factors of coarseness and obscurity.

Ethics could then be seen in terms of the symmetry between a man and his shadow. Conscience was the awareness of the need for symmetry; regret was no longer the cringing of a frightened criminal but the pain of a dislocated limb or the sorrow of an artist before a spoiled canvas; repentance and forgiveness could be understood. Only the rough calculus of humdrum morality would use the hesitant or precipitate choices of each hour.

This is a difficult and incomplete account of a preoccupation which lasted many months. Without the means of writing or of discovering what other people had thought, I could not save myself from rambling and from a certain eclectic dogmatism.

Words and ideas wandered slowly in an untidy scrawl across my brain, a kind of Brownian movement of particles in the mental fluid. The pattern of the movement was obscure, tending always to the limits of abstraction and blurred by the great fog of ignorance for which I had no lamp. Much of it was nonsense; much of it took me to Americas already thickly populated by earlier Columbuses; but I was happy with it for a while. In my earlier metaphor, I was content to be a mole, delighted that the surface of the earth was so great that there was no chance of my covering it all, careless of where I dug, and cheered by the occasional twinkling of a star. All I asked was the freedom and space to dig in.

Sometimes, as the winter deepened, I felt the cold and hunger so strongly that I assured myself that I would have to go to Germany at once, since it could only be less intolerable, but I was soon comforted by some new problem. And when my waistcoat was finished, I found myself at a loss for a physical occupation. I could not easily sit still for very long, but walking was now too energetic a distraction to be continued endlessly as in the old days. I added every useless embellishment to my handiwork of which I could think, but there was not unlimited scope, and I also needed it for its original purpose.

Then a sergeant came in one day with a prisoner orderly and asked me whether I would like to make Cellophane envelopes for bandages, a simple matter of folding and glueing. I rather pedantically began to refuse, on the grounds that I would not work for the enemy, but the orderly saw my intention and assured me that it was quite proper and that the work was considered neutral by the Red Cross. This excuse was enough for me to seize the chance of an unexacting pastime, and indeed it was hard to see what more sinister purpose could be served by such flimsy little bags; so I agreed.

I discovered that I am a bad maker of Cellophane envelopes. My folds were never quite straight, my glueing too generous, and my output negligible. For the first few days, the sergeant came round and patiently explained my shortcomings, surprising me because he took such trivial and voluntary work as seriously as if my life depended on it. When I showed no improvement he became fussy, although he once brought me an extra piece of bread as if to encourage me to greater things (or perhaps out of pure kindness, for he was a good man); but I at last became exasperated by his care for a precision which could not in my mind have the least importance, and I told him that I would do no more. He took it with the best humour, seeming relieved at the departure of a bad workman.

An Englishman came to No. 258 a few days before Christmas. I heard him calling me through his window and answered rather perfunctorily through my skylight, because I was happier without any intrusion and because talking through the skylight was a wearisome task. But he was so cheerful that I felt it would be surly of me not to respond to his friendliness. So I discovered who he was and that he had been transferred to solitary from a cell where he and his companion had bribed a guard to give them a German uniform. They had been found out, but when I listened to his story, which amused him endlessly, I reproached myself seriously with having remained supine for so many months with hardly a thought of attempting to escape.

Christmas opened with a barrage of greetings from No. 258, in more yeasty spirits than ever. Then my old sergeant from the top floor came round, and he, too, wished me a happy Christmas. He asked me if I wanted to attend Communion. I said no, and later regretted it, and finally did not regret it. The sergeant came again later bearing an enormous parcel from the Red Cross, containing all manner of sweetnesses. Then, when the soup came, a little packet was handed in with it: a piece of cooked pork from my neighbour. I feasted and was happy.

No. 258 was moved again soon afterwards. Many months later he was killed in Poland.

I resumed my peripatetic ways, but with a growing feeling of expectancy. The idea of leaving still filled me with horror, but I knew, with a sure intuition which made obstinacy vain, that it was time to go. This is the only fit expression, because it was the phrase which came to my mind at the time. As long as my brain worked, solitude served a purpose, but I could see that it was slowly exhausting the fuel with which it had started, and if it stopped from inanition I would have nothing left but cold and hunger, which would make short work of me. Metaphysics were not enough: they are an exercise, weakening rather than nourishing; and the brain requires food of real substance. *Dieu t'a fait pour l'aimer...*and He provided senses and a whole perceptible creation to that end.

But I was reluctant to leave. If my door was opened and I was told that I could go quietly wherever I liked, I would have gone with joy, but probably to some place where I knew nobody and would be able to remain aloof. But I could imagine the noise and promiscuity of a camp, and it repelled me.

I knew that so many months of solitude, though I had allowed them to torment me at times, had been in a sense an exercise in liberty. For, by absolving me from the need either to consider practical problems of living or to maintain the many unquestioned assumptions which cannot conveniently be abandoned in social life, I had been left free to drop the spectacles of the near-sighted and to scan the horizon of existence. And I believed that I had seen something there. But it was only a glimpse, a remote and tenuous apprehension of what lay behind the variety and activity of life, and I was afraid that I would lose sight of it as soon as I was forced to turn my attention back to my immediate surroundings.

Also I had built up a kind of security. The cell door was a battlement behind which I practised habits, and however futile they were they had become familiar from long and unvaried usage and represented an element of stability which was more desirable than even a hopeful hazard.

Nevertheless, the end came punctually. A sergeant came one morning and ordered me downstairs. I went unhappily, forgetting that I had once resigned myself and hoping only that I would soon be back.

On the ground floor I was put in a cell where there were already three other prisoners, all young and with their sociability quite unimpaired. They asked me all the ritual questions: Who was I? How long had I been there? Why was I arrested? And I answered with my own mixture of truth and untruth, although the muscles of my face rebelled, as if frozen with anaesthetic. I was willing to reciprocate their friendly curiosity, but could not, for I had no interest in their origins. I was only concerned with what they thought, but I could not broach the subject because I thought it quite probable that if I opened my mouth I should show myself to be mad. I therefore listened to their chatter and tried to recapture what evidently must be normality.

This cell and my companions in it were the threshold to the world of people and activity just as the cell in the rue des Saussaies had been the threshold to the world of solitude. My companions knew in some devious way where we were going: Royalieu, near Compiègne, and then to Germany; and I could hear the bustle and shouting outside as the convoy was collected and made ready. But I could not foresee what this new world would be like.

I could only look back to the thin faith I had acquired in my cell and know that it was to be put to the critical experiment, with my judgment distorted and weakened by more stresses than it could compensate at once, paralysed like a man at a railway junction with trains rushing towards him from all directions.

Then one of the Frenchmen gave me a cigarette, and the door opened, and we left.

We were formed up and marched into buses, which took us to Compiègne during the afternoon. I sat next to a Belgian dentist, who rejoiced in the temporary name of Pills. He had married in 1940, but after only ten days had sent his wife to Canada for safety and had not seen or heard from her since. Yet he showed no bitterness or doubt that after this last endurance he would be able to fetch her back and start again. I tried to talk to him and succeeded a little, but constantly had to check my tongue for fear of uttering some impossibility. There was a Belgian priest with us, too, and I wanted to try my questions out on him, but uncertainty overcame me.

I was mostly intent, however, upon seeing the world. The brown fields and grey skies of winter and the gaunt black trees were ineffably beautiful to me. My eyes could not adjust themselves to seeing such great spaces clearly, and the impression they gave me was not unlike that of a Chinese landscape, a beautiful haze broken by sparse but suddenly vivid detail. If the bus had stopped and let me out, I would perhaps have sat for hours on end gazing at some quite ordinary meadow. But the bus went on, and I was left bewildered by so vast and wonderful a scene.

We arrived at Compiègne near nightfall and were crowded together in a shed to spend the night there on the floor. The heaped and jostling bodies oppressed me, and the shouting and singing made me long for silence. But silence and privacy were gone; an episode was ended. Solitude, with its mysteries and adventures, had passed over me like a wave and washed back into the spreading ocean of the past, while the next sea, cold and clamorous, already mounted.

ⵜⵜ ⵜⵜ ⵉⵉⵉ

Afterword
by Hugh Purcell

Solitary Confinement and Buchenwald Concentration Camp

Christopher Burney ends *Solitary Confinement* with the sentence:

> Solitude, with its mysteries and adventures, had passed over me like a wave and washed back into the spreading ocean of the past, while the next sea, cold and clamorous, already mounted.

The first question that needs to be answered, then, is what happened to Burney after he left Fresnes prison? What was 'the next sea, cold and clamorous'?

In late January 1944, he was transported by train from the transit camp at Compiegne north of Paris to Buchenwald concentration camp outside Weimar near Leipzig. This meant surviving in a closed cattle wagon with very little food or water for four days and three nights. When he arrived at Buchenwald in the middle of the night, he had no idea what 'concentration camp' meant. Unlike Auschwitz, Buchenwald was not an extermination camp but a forced labour camp: its inmates were worked to death—nearly 60,000 between 1937 and 1945.

Burney stayed alive until liberation in April 1945, one of only a handful of British prisoners to survive. One reason was luck: near the end he hid undetected beneath floorboards in one of the prisoner blocks for forty-eight hours. Another was his job. His language skills, fluency in English and French and working knowledge of German and Spanish with some Russian enabled him to join the *lagerdolmetscher* or 'interpreter kommando'. This gave him freedom to move around within the camp and the opportunity to find extra warmth and food. Undoubtedly his character had something to do with it too. He was physically and mentally tough and he had leadership qualities based on an upper-class Scots arrogance. These all contributed to his survival, but an invaluable asset were the psychological defences from the seventeen months he had spent in solitary confinement in Fresnes.

In the 1970s, the Department of Adult Psychiatry at the Medical Academy in Krakow published the results of its ten-year study of a hundred or so survivors of concentration and extermination camps. To sum up their findings they coined the phrase 'K-Z syndrome' ('Konzentrationslager'). One conclusion was unequivocal:

> The initiation into the camp hell was a shock that was stronger than any other trauma of human life. All authors dealing with the concentration camps emphasise the initial reaction to imprisonment which was generally experienced, and which led to death in many prisoners. A prisoner had to adjust to camp life within the first several weeks or months, otherwise he had to die.

The question was how to adjust?

> Firstly, prisoners had to become indifferent to everything that was going on around them, had to withdraw into their internal world. This defensive insensitivity was referred to as 'camp autism'.[1]

Burney had practised Fresnes 'autism' for the previous eighteen months. He had learned to suppress not only the physical agonies of cold and hunger but also the psychological agonies of claustrophobia, loneliness and fear. He had come out the other side. As he wrote in his memorable conclusion to *Solitary Confinement*:

> I knew that so may months of solitude, though I had allowed them to torment me at times, had been in a sense an exercise in liberty. For by absolving me from the need either to consider practical problems of living or to maintain the many unquestioned assumptions which cannot conveniently be abandoned in social life, I had been left free to drop the spectacles of the near-sighted and to scan the horizon of existence.

Remarkable though it may seem, Burney's friends in Buchenwald remarked on his 'serenity' and this was due to his unintentional training in Fresnes. On his last night in Buchenwald after the camp's liberation by the American army on 12 April 1945, he lay awake and examined his feelings: 'I was not drunk with freedom—freedom of movement, freedom from want—for I had in some way trained myself to be spiritually free, and when that is achieved the other "freedoms" become less noticeable.'

---

1   Kępiński, A. 'The so-called "KZ-Syndrome": An attempt at a synthesis'. *Medical Review – Auschwitz*. August 21, 2017. Originally published as 'Tzw. "KZ-syndrom". Próba syntezy.' *Przegląd Lekarski – Oświęcim*. 1970: 18–23.

The authors of the 'K-Z Syndrome' study identified a second necessity for survival. Once withdrawn into a private world, the state of 'camp autism', the prisoner needed 'a solid point of reference', most usually a faith:

> [A prisoner] had to withdraw into his internal life and find a solid point of reference there, such as faith in survival, the conviction that even the greatest evil must end one day, thoughts of family, religious faith, or thoughts about the punishment of the persecutors.

Burney did not have a belief that he would survive but he did have a religious faith that good would triumph over evil. He describes in *Solitary Confinement* how he came to this conclusion after weeks of mental cogitation as he paced up and down his cell:

> If, as I believed, the only absolute was God, and good by definition, there could be no such *thing* as evil: all it could be was an epithet meaning 'less than good'.

Burney thought that the polar opposites of good and evil should be replaced by a scale which would all be positive degrees of good. All aspects of life formed a spectrum that all originated from a single source.

> Such a change in the scale of values does not entail much revision of the grosser forms of judgment. Things and actions will still be good or bad. But it does accompany a change of attitude: pessimism becomes optimism, and the good of life is no longer overshadowed by its imperfections. Henceforth, the tiniest window bringing light will always dominate the bleak and oppressive walls and passages beyond them. And we will fight for what we love instead of pursuing what we hate.

Of course, a cell locks out as well as locks in; there is no outside world to combat so the demons are within its four walls and within the mind. In contrast, in Buchenwald, the world of the 'Konzentrationslager', described by Burney in one word as 'disgusting', was scarcely bearable and Burney's new faith was tested to breaking point. 'The death of despair gnawed at my heart' is how he put it in the intensely personal *Letter from Buchenwald* which he wrote in the freezing winter of 1944/5, leaving the camp with it in the lining of his clothing. It prompts the essential question, enquiring beneath the barest outline of his wartime career– who was Christopher Burney? Without a knowledge of his life before he was thrown into Fresnes and then Buchenwald, we cannot properly appreciate *Solitary Confinement*.

Solitary Confinement and Burney's Upbringing

Christopher was born in England in 1917 and spent his childhood years in India where his father, Jack, was serving as a Colonel in the Royal Artillery. He and his brother were sent back England to a conventional prep school in 1926, and their parents joined them a few years later. Then, in 1931, the tragedy occurred that became the most formative event in the life of the young Christopher. He watched his father, whom he adored, die before his eyes.

Christopher was thirteen and the family was sitting round the tea table when Jack suddenly suffered a heart attack and was dead within moments. The effect on Christopher was traumatic and enduring. He had always shown a wild and wilful spirit and now he had no restraining influence on him. He hated the stepfather his mother, Dorothy, married for convenience and she could not control him.

The big row came two years later when Christopher was at Wellington College. He was clever, so his headmaster wanted him to study classics with the intention of going to Oxford. He wanted none of this. He wished to study languages and then follow his father into the Royal Artillery by studying to be an army officer at Sandhurst. When he was not permitted to have his own way, he ran away from school. He was just sixteen.

Between 1934 and 1939 he wandered round Europe, living 'miserably', wrote Dorothy, in Switzerland, Spain, and Paris before returning to England and moving from job to job in London. Had his father been alive to offer strong paternal guidance, Christopher may well have stayed at school, progressed to Oxford or Cambridge universities, and then found a more conventional way to serve in the war than being dropped into France as a secret agent. On the other hand, through his time in Europe, he became fluent in French and acquired a working knowledge of Spanish and Russian, and these languages would later save his life. He also satisfied his need for independence, and even if he was in dire circumstances much of the time, this was a preparation for the future, too.

However, he also received no academic education after the age of sixteen. He knew nothing about the arts or sciences except what he taught himself. It is important in understanding *Solitary Confinement* to know that Burney had only a small core of academic knowledge to draw on in his endless searching for enlightenment. Bear in mind, too, that apart from a copy of the Bible given him in his second year in Fresnes, he had no other books and no paper, pencil or person to aid his pondering. He admits:

> Words and ideas wandered slowly in an untidy scrawl across my brain. The pattern of the movement was obscure, tending always to the limits of abstraction and blurred by the great fog of ignorance for which I had no lamp. Much of it [my thinking] was nonsense.

He encountered an intellectual obstacle too. Although his belief in God was 'incoherent but unyielding', he found much of the

Bible irrational if not contradictory. This, he said, nearly drove him mad: 'This seemingly insoluble antagonism between belief and reason threatened to explode in insanity.' Many of us concur in this view but few have to endure the solitude that causes such arguments to nag at one's mind.

Burney found a kindred spirit in Shakespeare's *Richard II*, and he used this quotation as the preface to *Solitary Confinement*. It is a difficult quotation that many minds with much more training than Christopher's have wrestled with. It appears in Act V, Scene 5, when King Richard is a prisoner in Pomfret Castle:

> For no thought is contented. The better sort,
> As thoughts of things divine, are intermix'd
> With scruples, and do set the word itself
> Against the word:
> As thus—*Come little ones*, and then again—
> *It is as hard to come, as for a camel*
> *To thread the postern of a small needle's eye.*

So far, so comprehensible. The quotation continues with language that is obviously significant, even if its meaning is speculative:

> Thoughts tending to ambition, they do plot
> Unlikely wonders; how these vain weak nails
> May tear a passage through the flinty ribs
> Of this hard world, my ragged prison walls:
> And for they cannot, die in their own pride.

Does this mean that in Burney's mind, understanding contradictory thoughts of, for example, belief contending with reason, were limited by the poverty of his imprisoned mind and they could not break free? That such frustration was like trying to tear a passage through rough prison walls with weak fingernails? And since there was no hope of these contradictions being resolved they died before they went any further? The literary critic Frank Kermode wrote in *The Sense of an Ending* that these verses from Richard II made 'exquisite sense' to him after reading *Solitary Confinement*.

Solitary Confinement and Julia

Christopher Burney dedicated the book to his wife Julia, an invisible presence in *Solitary Confinement*. His ten-page *Letter from Buchenwald* was intended for Julia. In it, he recalls the intimate times they had shared together, particularly the walks in the Black Mountains behind the Burney family home at Hay on Wye in the Welsh border country, walks that Julia described in her own memoir as representing 'all that was secret and good and eternal.' He wrote 'I know that I still love you and sometimes through the cold and hunger I feel the lack of you more than anything else.'

Christopher met Julia Burrell in the summer of 1941 in Ayrshire, Scotland, where he was training with 12 Commando. They shared Scots upper class parentage for he was descended from the Burney family of literary and military fame and she was the daughter of the wealthy Scots family that set up the international Burrell Art Collection in Glasgow. In fact, despite his birth and upbringing, Christopher always regarded himself as Scottish. They soon fell in love.

After Christopher left on his mission to France in 1942 and disappeared without trace for nearly three years, she wrote to him continually and remained loyal. He never received her letters but some of them, mysteriously, survived and after Christopher's death in 1980, Julia returned to them in the memoir she wrote about their time together. Her memoir is a tale of tragic romance but also an important source of information about the post-traumatic stress that consumed his later years. An extract from her memoir gives the flavour of their romance.

By serving as interpreter for the American Sixth Army that liberated Buchenwald, Christopher was able to cadge an airlift back to London within days. On the morning of 16 April 1945, Julia was at her desk in the Secret Intelligence Service (MI6) headquarters at Westminster where she worked as a secretary when the phone rang:

There was a pause, and then Christopher's voice said 'Julia?' I suppose I said 'Yes.'

'Can you have lunch with me today?' I must have said 'Yes.'

'Where shall we meet?' Without thinking, I gave my usual reply to a lunchtime invitation: 'St. James's tube station at 1 o'clock.'

'I'll be there.'

I put the telephone down and then the awful truth dawned that in my haste and excitement, I had committed myself to a three hour wait before I could see him again after such a long time.

When at last we did meet, we stood in front of each other and exchanged a perfunctory kiss. I did not notice he was wearing a strange assortment of clothes; an army battledress top, thin grey flannel trousers over which were pulled home-made Wellington boots. His head had been shaved, but long enough ago to have grown a moleskin skullcap of short hair. His face was as bloated and as white as a dandelion puff. I noticed none of this; I only knew I was in his element and that I was in Heaven.

'Where have you been?' I asked, breaking a long silence.

'It will take time to tell.' Pause. 'Are you married?'

'No.'

[They went for lunch in her flat in nearby Marsham Court].

In the little kitchen I began to peel potatoes. My hands were trembling so badly that I was taking half the potato with the skin.

'Look out!' Christopher shouted, 'You're wasting food.' For someone whose diet had been rotten mangelwurzels, a potato was a precious luxury. We were both in emotional shock.

The Writing of Solitary Confinement

Christopher and Julia married on 2 February 1946. By this time he had finished writing what became the companion book to *Solitary Confinement*. *Dungeon Democracy* covers the fifteen months after Fresnes when Burney was in Buchenwald. It is a short book of 40,000 words and he wrote it in just three or four months. It was first published in 1945, six years before *Solitary Confinement* (in 1984 they were republished together in one volume by Macmillan). *Dungeon Democracy* was the first description of a concentration camp that many readers had encountered.

They are very different books in style and form and purpose, and in quality, too. Christopher wrote *Dungeon Democracy* in a hurry. Just returned from what he called 'a living hell', he wrote with a mission, to tell the world about concentration camps and to warn that unless the degradation of humanity could be stopped 'it will mean back to Buchenwald for me and a maiden trip for most of you.'

He wrote in a mood of heightened emotion. The transition within weeks from piling up corpses to sitting quietly in a London study could not be achieved without trauma. Christopher was in a state, having lost a third of his weight and startling Julia with his 'pathetic little chalk white face with eyes as black and shiny as wet coal'. He was disturbed though not yet showing symptoms of post traumatic stress, and it shows in the tone of *Dungeon Democracy*, particularly in its conclusion.

His depression about the lack of humanity he witnessed in Buchenwald, 'the amorality, the cowed seeking of refuge in a herd, the bitterness and longing for revenge (on anybody), the leadership of the animal emotions' was increased by his deep repugnance of Germans. He analysed what he called 'the illness of mass-Germanism'. News of the world beyond Buchenwald, of the discovery of extermination camps, of millions of refugees wandering Europe seeking a home, of countless little wars still continuing, must have depressed Christopher further. Europe was still a savage continent.

Dungeon Democracy, then, is memorable for its account of how a concentration camp operated and of how he survived, but his call for a moral reformation seems dated now and its tone of heightened emotion is understandable but hard to take. Burney told his publisher and friend Alan Maclean that he wrote it in too much of a hurry and he was dissatisfied with it.

Solitary Confinement is very different. Burney wrote the book with great care. He spent five years meticulously trying not to 'distort the balance of truth' between exaggeration and underestimate. As he expressed it in one of his carefully balanced sentences in the preface to the second edition published in 1961, 'The experience of unpleasantness is as exaggerated in the second-hand reading as it is dimmed in the first hand remembering.' Further, he tried as far as possible to eliminate afterthoughts and describe what he felt at the time, not easy after a gap of several years. Then there was his awareness that he could not possibly paint the whole picture in any detail because, as he put it in an unforgettable sentence, 'there was so much total emptiness between the actions as to make it resemble an astronomer's description of the universe.'

Along with his endless cogitations about the meaning of good and evil, Burney was analysing the meaning of an autobiographical experience. What was a true recollection? When was it true and in what detail? This is part of what makes *Solitary Confinement* such a privilege to read.

A British audience was first made aware of Christopher Burney and his solitary confinement by the talk he gave on the BBC Home Service in January 1946, rebroadcast two months later. Immediately after, he and Julia flew off to New York. She wrote 'the cinema organ played at full throttle as we flew, hand in hand, into the sunset of a promised land, unmarked by war, where hearts were warm and food unrationed.' As a result of *Dungeon Democracy*, Christopher had been invited to join the secretariat of the new United Nations based in New York and here they lived for the next four years. This is where he wrote *Solitary Confinement*.

The Publication of *Solitary Confinement*

By 1951 he was back in London with Julia and their two young children. *Solitary Confinement* was published the following year with a foreword by the poet and playwright Christopher Fry:

> No man is free who will not dare to pursue the questions of his own loneliness. It is through them that he lives. The stature of this book is best distilled in one sentence from it 'I knew that so many months of solitude, though I had allowed them to torment me at times, had been in a sense an exercise in liberty.'

Despite the merits of *Solitary Confinement* its first publication was a failure. The publishers, Clerke and Cockeran, were new and poor. The day of publication, they rang Christopher and told him not to cash their cheque for £50 because they had gone bankrupt. The print run was small, the book made no impact and was soon unobtainable. Like Christopher in Fresnes, it disappeared without trace.

Nine years later, it was republished, this time by Macmillan. Its reception was completely different. It became a *cause celebre*. The prestigious *Times Literary Supplement* devoted its first leader to the event, under the title OUT OF PRINT:

> It is cheering when a book of real quality seems to break through a barrier of indifference and bad luck. Ten years ago, Mr Christopher Burney wrote a short work called *Solitary Confinement* which is one of the classics both of the last war and of that long process

174

of imprisonment, brutality and sudden death in which the war itself was only one extra acute and well publicised stage.

Yesterday it was re-issued in a new edition by another publisher and here it is once more with its singular balance of contemplativeness and self-ridicule, of the philosophical, the religious and the urgently physical, of spiritual gropings and the sharp, vivid, glimpses of the outside world; all clearly and detachedly described. It seems possible that the hibernation has done it no harm. The book's depth and range of reference are more evident than before; that richness which is there to be dug into not only by ordinary readers but by philosophers, psychologists and priests who want to see their ideas tested by an intelligent and sensitive individual in an extreme state.

Alerted by the *Times Literary Supplement*, many newspapers and journals carried reviews. They were unanimous in their praise. 'One of the most remarkable and moving books to come from the last war,' wrote *John O'London's Weekly*, then 'the leading literary review in the British Empire' and this review set the tone. Many reviewers remarked on its literary and spiritual qualities. The *Sunday Times* had a clever sentence; 'This ordinary, intelligent man (who also happens to write excellently) begins to discover solitary confinement to be an exercise in liberty, and the imminence of death a penetration of life.' In the *Sunday Telegraph* Rebecca West, whom *Time* magazine dubbed 'indisputably the world's number one woman writer', wrote, 'Readers who are genuinely inquisitive about their own souls, and other people's, and (these being as they are) about the prospects for our species, should read *Solitary Confinement.*' This line certainly helped sell the book.

The originator of this *cause celebre* was Alan Maclean, then an editor with Macmillan and Co. He had become friends with the Burneys during the 1950s and stayed with them at weekends, sheltering from the infamy of being the brother of the Communist spy Donald Maclean, who had defected to the Soviet Union in 1951. Maclean pushed for it to be republished in 1961 as 'a classic work which will illuminate the minds of its readers for years to come'. Two decades later, in 1984, four years after Christopher's death, he decided that Macmillan's should publish *Solitary Confinement* in a single volume with *Dungeon Democracy*. In his introduction to that edition, Maclean wrote, 'The books themselves differ equally in tone, scope, form and purpose but they belong together on one volume as if they were the two dissimilar sides of the same coin.'

Solitary Confinement as a Literary Work

Soon after *Solitary Confinement* was published in 1961, it was noticed by the Italian publisher Roberto Calasso. He wanted it for a series in his new Milan publishing house, Adelphi Edizioni, to be called Biblioteca. Years later, in his book *The Art of the Publisher*, he described the sort of books he was looking for. They had to be about 'a singular experience, about something that happened to the author on a particular occasion...and has been put into writing'. The author may not have written before, nor perhaps again, but 'that work (that singular book) had gone through him in order to come into existence'.

Calasso then made the obvious point that no experience, in itself, was enough to bring a good book into existence. There were many cases of fascinating and significant events in the last war about, for example, imprisonment, deportation and torture, which had become 'dull books'. He was not interested in these, however singular. 'But for a clear and simple account of the experience of total isolation and total defencelessness and how it can yield a discovery of something else, the book to read is *Solitary Confinement* by Christopher Burney.' And so, it became number 18 in the Biblioteca series.

Following Macmillan's 1984 edition, *Solitary Confinement* fell out of print in English, and in 2006, Brad Bigelow featured it on his Neglected Books website, which draws attention to books of quality that have been 'neglected, overlooked, forgotten, or stranded by changing tides in critical or popular taste'. 'What makes *Solitary Confinement* stand out among war and prison memoirs,' Bigelow wrote, 'is that Burney focuses, to the exclusion of almost all extraneous details, on the mental and emotional experience of his long stretch in solitary.' In the years since that post, other readers shared their personal associations with *Solitary Confinement*:

> 'I just learned of it through Roberto Calasso's newly translated and published *The Art of the Publisher*, for it was one of the books he decided first to publish, what he refers to as a "singular book".'

> 'I first read this fairly soon after the war, and I've re read it so often that the spine is almost off, but the paper and type cannot be damaged by age and fit the contents in their austerity.'

> 'When I stand in front of my bookshelves wondering what to read next, I often find the spine of Burney's book calling out to me: "Forget the rest: I am in a class of my own."'

> 'This is a truly remarkable book. I came across it in a church on Clapham Common some twenty-five years ago, amongst a few dog-eared paperbacks you could take away with you for a few pence. I was arrested by the title and myself leading a solitary brooding life at the time—though by choice not, as in his case, necessity. It is simply and powerfully written by an educated man who could easily have made it much more erudite (and pretentious) had he wanted : this is the truth, nothing but the truth, at any rate as near as he remembers it.

Get this book from the Library, buy it from Amazon, but READ THIS BOOK and life will never seem the same again.'

These days the subject of solitary confinement has been studied and described by penologists, criminologists, psychologists, sociologists, lawyers, journalists and victims themselves. As the death sentence has been abolished in many countries and most American states, solitary confinement for life has come to be seen as the more common (but still inhuman) form of punishment. According to the Bureau of Justice Statistics, over 80,000 persons are held in solitary confinement in the USA alone, and in the so-called 'supermax' prisons where the sentence is sometimes for life, thousands of inmates are held in near-total isolation, with just one hour for exercise and ablutions a day. This treatment has spawned its own diagnosis, 'SHU syndrome' for Special Housing Unit or Security Housing Unit. 'SHU syndrome' is classified as a 'major, clinically distinguishable psychiatric syndrome'. Similar forms of solitary confinement are in place worldwide, and numerous groups such as 'Unlock the Box' and 'Solitary Watch' protest about its use.

In Christopher Burney's case, he was not so much sentenced to solitary confinement as discarded, thrown away into a prison cell until he would be either taken out and executed or transported to die in a concentration camp. He had no release, even for one hour a day and no provision of clothing, exercise, or supervised diet. But his book is testimony to the inhuman effects of extreme isolation as punishment.

There are countless first-hand descriptions of penal solitary confinement in journals and on the Internet, but these are not written for literary merit. That is to say that they are not written to reveal a mental and emotional experience leading to, in Roberto Callaso's phrase, 'the discovery of something else' which lies at the heart of *Solitary Confinement*. Burney left school under-educated, but he showed rare literary ability to achieve this.

For a more recent account of solitary confinement that relates with similar eloquence the inner torture it causes, we should turn to *An Evil Cradling* by the Irishman Brian Keenan. Keenan was a writer working at the American University in Beirut in 1986 when he was kidnapped and held hostage by Islamic Jihad in retaliation for the American involvement in the civil war in Lebanon. He was kept in solitary confinement for several months and then spent the next four years, much of the time blindfolded, sharing a cell with the journalist John McCarthy. In *An Evil Cradling*, he describes how during his solitary confinement he broke down, lost all self control and suffered extreme agitation. He panicked, felt lost, abandoned:

> I am thrust suddenly into agonies of tears. The world has forgotten me, has no meaning for me...I am bereft even of God. I am a bag of flesh and scrape, a heap of offal tossed unwanted into the corner of this filthy room. Even the filth has more life, more significance than I have.
>
> I have ceased being, ceased becoming. Even banging my head against the wall does not retrieve me to myself. Many times, I think of death, pray for it, look for it, chase after its rapturous kiss. But I have come to a point of such nothingness that even death cannot be. I have no more weeping.

Did Burney suffer the 'extreme anxiety, depression, paranoia and psychosis', described by Keenan, that make up the definition of the SHU syndrome? In his *Letter from Buchenwald*, Burney writes how, when he was at his lowest, he experienced similar agonies in Fresnes:

> The depth of despair gnawing at my heart and of insanity at my brain...the loneliness and tedium and impotence, till sometimes one felt death would be better...the passing of many days and nights and weeks when all hope left me and I saw myself only in the present, starving, emotionally bottled up and going mad in spasms.

These extreme and intimate descriptions of suffering, however, do not find their way into *Solitary Confinement*. Did his mood when he wrote that *Letter from Buchenwald* exaggerate his descriptions? Or did the descriptions fail his test, when writing *Solitary Confinement*, 'not to distort the balance of truth'? Perhaps he was 'emotionally bottled up' and never did suffer the extreme symptoms of SHU. Or perhaps the stiff upper lip of a Scotsman writing in the 1950s prevented him from going there.

Christopher Burney's stubborn refusal to focus on despair is what ultimately makes *Solitary Confinement* an inspirational work. But that attitude came at a cost. I would like to close by to quoting Alan Maclean's final words from his introduction to the 1984 edition of *Solitary Confinement* and *Dungeon Democracy*:

> His qualities of mind and character will be evident to anyone who reads these books. They didn't change, but the price of survival was high and his health, like that of many other survivors, deteriorated remorselessly over the last twenty years of his life. He found no comfort in the practices of the established Churches and religions, and he never lost his mistrust of established authority. Heroes are made of awkward stuff. Very seldom to they find in the circumstances of their heroism a light to lighten their darkness, and even less seldom do they have the literary skills and insights to depict it in writing.

Maclean concludes with what serves (to me) as Christopher's epitaph:

> I don't think he ever found again the serenity of spirit, composure of thought and the simple faith which he fashioned and earned in Fresnes. But he never forgot it and nor should we.

Descent from Ararat

In 1962 Macmillan published Burney's third and last book, *Descent from Ararat*, and in 1980, Alan Maclean included a shorter (and better) version in the *Winter's Tale 26* anthology, along with stories and essays by writers such as Nadine Gordimer, Edna O'Brien, and Beryl Bainbridge. This is the version reprinted in this volume. Maclean wrote that the book 'defies classification' and reviewers variously called it 'a parable', 'an allegory' or 'a fable'. Burney said, simply, that it was 'a story'. I believe that it is an important piece of writing both because it shows the state of Burney's worsening post traumatic stress and because it repeats, eloquently, his philosophy of life honed in *Solitary Confinement*.

The story is simplicity itself. A man recovers consciousness on a narrow ledge below the top of a mountain to find a rescuer beside him. The injured man has lost his memory and is told by his rescuer that he was attempting suicide. He has no knowledge why he is there. They shelter for the night on the mountain and spend the time in discourse about the loss of memory, suicide, good, evil and the existence of God. In the early morning the rain stops and a rainbow appears (a clear reference to the Biblical story of Noah's Ark). The stranger helps the injured man down the mountain and then goes his own way. Inspired by the rainbow, the beauty of the countryside below and the exhortation from the stranger to 'plant a vineyard' and enjoy a long life (as did Noah), the injured man delivers himself to the care of a doctor.

It is clear to me, though not to any of the original book's reviewers, that the injured man and the stranger are both Christopher Burney, his ego and his alter ego. He is trying to persuade himself, through his alter ego, that despite his severe post-traumatic stress, his life is worth living: that his memory will return, that suicide is 'not a logical solution to a problem' and that 'the only important thing for you is to be absolutely sure that you are.

Don't even try to see yourself *as* anything. Just be.'

While still on the mountain, sheltering from the storm in a little hollow, the stranger (alter ego) expands on this: 'Learn to be content that you are; that is the first truth. Remind yourself that the intangibles you perceive when you are most conscious of being are the first realities. God, wonder, beauty, love, generosity—a mixed bag but that's because of the language they are put into. They are still the elements of life.'

The injured man asks the stranger if he believes in God? 'No', he answers, 'I think I know him a little…something I'm aware of like I'm aware of being. It's nothing I can explain rationally. In the long run, though, I just have to sit quietly and stop arguing, as you sit under a summer sky. Then I can consent to everything without any violence to my reason.'

In 1963, the year after *Descent from Ararat* was first published, Burney suffered what he called 'a nervous breakdown'. The immediate trigger was his listening to Benjamin Britten's *War Requiem*, which its composer dedicated to Roger, Christopher's younger brother, who drowned in a mysterious submarine sinking in 1942. After the attack, Julia wrote to Britten that Christopher's breakdown was 'an affliction so terrible it defies description.' In fact, it was the latest of numerous severe bouts of depression, nightmares and panic attacks over preceding years, leading sometimes to catatonic collapse. This was in line with the 'KZ syndrome' that showed post-traumatic stress as a result of the concentration camp experience to be a progressive condition that eventually engulfed over seventy-five percent of survivors.

Shortly after his attack, Christopher abandoned his wife and teenage children and went to live alone in France, ending up in a remote village in Normandy. In 1976, he returned to London and was partially reconciled with Julia, but he still lived alone with his demons. In December 1980, he died while sitting in the library of The Traveller's Club. Alan Maclean wrote that 'few of his wartime colleagues would have forecast such a peaceful exit', but the conditions of his death denied the tragedy of his last years. Julia wrote that 'his depression deprived him of love, for me and for God, and his misery was profound.'

The stranger on the mountain disappears from sight after his final words: 'I hope you remember to look at rainbows'. But in Christopher Burney's own life, the optimism of his alter ego was no match for the sufferings of his ego. *Descent from Ararat* remains as an eloquent testimony to the beliefs he struggled to formulate as he paced his cell in Fresnes. Here they are expressed in a form of Socratic dialogue, so in his later years Burney may at least have consoled himself with the philosopher's dictum that 'the unexamined life is not worth living.'

꒐꒐꒐

Descent from Ararat

by Christopher Burney

卌

When I returned to consciousness my head seemed quite clear but curiously empty, like a smoke-room freshly aired. My senses were functioning, and I could see and hear clearly, but the impressions they made were unusually distinct and direct, like raindrops falling on a window-pane instead of on grass. Their impact was not muffled by being absorbed into the sponge of memory, where they would be fused and muddled with all the other impressions of the years. I did not think I had lost my memory, only that it seemed to be isolated from the present. I seemed, on reflection, to know a great deal: that I was lying rather precariously on the side of a mountain, that a man was standing over me, that he was dressed in what I thought of as grey tweed and shod in what I knew to be shepherd's boots. But of myself, my name, my past, I could recall nothing—or, rather, *did* recall nothing, because I was not even moved to make the effort. I had escaped from my memory. If I had lost it, I could not have thought with words or understood the man when he spoke, and in this I had no difficulty.

It was just that my memory was no longer about *me*.

I had been looking about me for a minute or two, though without moving, when the man spoke.

'We shall have to spend the night out here,' he said. 'I am pretty sure your ankle's not broken, but it's quite badly sprained, and I should never be able to get you down before nightfall.'

Involuntarily, I wriggled my feet and realised for the first time that, indeed, my left ankle was hurting badly.

'Even if I went down alone,' he went on, 'I couldn't get back with help till early morning. You were so careful not to be noticed this morning when you were coming up the valley that no one will think of sending a party out to look for you. And no one will miss me in the time. So we'd better make the best of it. It's going to rain, but there's a little cave I noticed on the way up. It's only about three hundred feet below us and we should be all right there for one night. I'll see you down in the morning.'

It was cold already. We were high up, on a narrow shelf about fifty feet from the top of a precipice which formed one face of the summit and dropped sheer below us for some hundreds of feet. In front of us lay a whole mountain kingdom of green and brown and grey and white; behind us, the summit which ruled it, and beyond that again, presumably, the valley to the lowlands.

I was preoccupied with relating this scene and, above all, the man's words to myself. I could see where I was plainly enough, and the name of the mountain or even the country had not enough importance to become a question. I could understand his plan, but only in the sense that I took it for granted that what he said was right and would happen. But when he spoke about following *me*, or about *my* having done this or that, I felt rather as one does towards old men who tell you stories of their childhood, to which you have no relevance at all. I said to myself in a distinctly formal way that I should say something back to him, but he appeared not to want me to speak.

'I might not have noticed you myself,' he went on, sitting down beside me, 'but something about you told me that you were going to kill yourself. I suppose I recognised it instinctively, because, after all, I couldn't really know anything about you. Anyway, I followed you.

'I kept well behind you, as far as I could, until you were nearly on the top. I don't know whether it was out of respect for your privacy, or out of curiosity, or because I thought that if you felt like that it would be better for you in the long run actually to see the brink. I didn't let you out of sight, though. Sometimes you went very fast, as if you were determined to get there at all costs, pushing yourself along, and at others you seemed almost to stop, as if you had driven yourself beyond the limits. It was difficult not to run into you on the corners when you did that. But when you got to the top there I wished I had stopped you earlier. I didn't know what to do. I was terrified that if you saw me or if I shouted to you, you might throw yourself over in sheer panic. Then I saw this shelf underneath you, so I crawled out on to it and shouted for help.'

This stirred memory of a sort in me. I could picture the cliff-top and a call for help and the body of a man lying just below. But it seemed to me that the body was mine. Of course, it was mine at this moment, but I could not remember getting there. I paid careful but disinterested attention to what the man said as he went on.

'I thought that if you saw me here it might shock you out of whatever you were thinking about. Perhaps you would instinctively go to help someone in distress, but more likely I thought that you would feel, so to speak, ridiculed if you found that someone else had apparently done what you intended to do and had only ended up squealing for help. Bathos is a great help to realism. Anyway, you came. You slipped and fell just as you got here and that's what sprained your ankle. Then you passed out. We've been here nearly two hours, but I couldn't possibly have got you off here alone.'

It is a very curious sensation to have someone describe the actions of someone else to you as if he were talking about you.

There was no possible connection in my mind between a person who had recently wanted to throw himself off the cliff and me. All I could see was that I was indeed here with a bad ankle. I looked over the edge to where, far below, the precipice eased off into a slope of scree, and quickly drew back so that I pressed against the rock behind me. I had never liked steep drops, I knew, and the thought of willingly looking, let alone launching myself, over this one was empty and cold and impossible. At the bottom of the scree there was a dark place where the light did not reach, and as I glimpsed it my brain seemed to become like it, black and empty.

At last I managed to speak, but even my voice came out strangely and I could not positively say it was my own.

'I'm afraid I've lost my memory,' I said, and could manage no more.

'Good Heavens!' he said. 'Don't worry about that. You're not concussed, since you didn't hit your head on anything, so you've just stopped remembering about yourself. Probably it had become too unpleasant. Brains are very efficient and on the whole co-operative. So don't be in too much of a hurry to start remembering again. I rather envy you.'

'But you tell me that I was going to commit suicide. You even seem absolutely sure of it. But it doesn't mean anything to me at all. I can't even bear the thought of falling over the edge. But since I can't remember even coming here I can't say it's not true, either.'

It was curious talking like this, hunched up on a ledge so narrow that we hardly dared turn to look at each other.

'You must not worry about me,' he said. 'After I leave you in the morning we are not likely to meet again, and I am not in the least curious about what brought you up here. I know you aren't a maniac, because if you had been you would not have paused when you got to the top of the precipice. You wouldn't even have heard me call. I should have been sorry about that, but there would have been nothing I could do.

'Were you trying to make a gesture? No, I don't think so. People who do that choose public places as a rule. They are not really trying to commit suicide. They dramatise themselves and their misfortunes and, so to speak, write one scene too many. I think they hope that a rescuer will appear in it and then all their injustices will be recognised and they can have a new life in which they will be appreciated and cherished. But the rescuer doesn't always come along. Poor people! When they die, as they so often do, we should call it accidental death rather than suicide. After all, the word is used terribly loosely. All sorts of perfectly happy people, especially in war, are said to do something *suicidal*, when all they've done is to sacrifice their own lives in order to save other people's. Captain Oates wasn't lost or bewildered or unhappy. He wasn't trying to solve any internal problem of his own by going off into the blizzard. He was simply making it possible for his friends to survive when he knew that he hadn't much chance anyway.'

He paused for quite a long time and, although I could not see his face, I felt he was frowning in reflection. Eventually he went on:

'Ordinary lunatics sometimes kill themselves, too, but I think that's mostly by accident. You stay sane as long as your brain makes something comprehensible out of what it takes in. If it tried to deal with everything it would make nonsense of it, so it has its own built-in system with which it either rejects what it can't make out or simply waves it aside, as it were, and invents an excuse for things being as they are. You'd be surprised, if you thought about it, how much so-called philosophy is really inventing plausible excuses.

'In a way, your brain behaves like your ears. When the noise gets too bad, then you go mad by degrees. The safety-valves go wrong and the whole system blows up. I think a lot of what we call lunatics are people whose logical system has changed so as to make the intake of information tolerable. Maybe it will go so haywire that you'll think a lake is a cup of tea, and then you'll drown, but surely that must be an accident rather than deliberate self-destruction.'

'So you don't think I'm mad, either?' I asked.

'No,' he said, 'I'd be very surprised if you were.'

'Then why do you feel so sure I was going to commit suicide? I'll grant you it may be looked on as an accident in a lot of cases, but if you exclude maniacs and self-dramatists and plain lunatics what's left?'

'I'll tell you in a moment,' he said, 'but I think we ought to move to our cave. It will be easier to talk and we must make sure of getting to it while the sun is still up. The first few yards are going to be difficult, but if you give me your left hand and let me go first we ought to be alright. But try not to let your bad foot give way or we'll not be able to discuss anything anymore.'

He stood up carefully and I did the same, only more carefully, feeling up the rock-face with my fingers. We had to face to our left, which made my right foot, the one on which I had to put my weight, the one nearest the edge. I tried and retried it before I straightened the leg, afraid that the edge would crumble. And I made my neck almost stiff by concentrating on looking upward.

I stumbled where the shelf petered out to a bare foothold, just before it reached the shoulder which marked the end of the precipice. I tried to regain my balance with my right foot, but there was no room for it, and I felt my arm jerked almost out of my shoulder as my guide, who was himself still a good yard from safety, gripped my wrist and threw himself forward. For a fraction of a second I was in mid-air and felt all the blood leave my head, but then my sprained ankle gave in to necessity and took hold again, and with a final heave we found ourselves lying on the comparatively easy slope.

He said nothing, but watched me carefully as I got to my feet again, and we went slowly across and down the slope until we came to a little hollow under an overhang. 'Cave' seemed to me a big word for what we had, which was little more than an eyrie sheltered from above, scarcely deeper than a saucer and with only a few small rocks to keep off the wind which had now risen considerably and was scouring the mountain-side. He arranged these as best he could and we sat in their small lee.

I watched him as he arranged himself into a hump, so that he exposed the least possible surface to the wind, but what I saw told me almost nothing. Physically, apart from his obvious hardi-ness, he was indeterminate. As to age, height, build I have been unable to manufacture a description which satisfies me. They were all middling, but there was nothing middling or indeed on any scale about the total. Simplicity seemed to have been carried so far in everything about him, in dress and voice and movement, as to defy the complications of comparison. He looked at me simply, too, neither kindly nor with authority, neither shyly nor keenly, making me an object of regard rather than of inspection.

'I wonder why we regard lunatics with such horror,' he said, 'as if they were some sort of living dead. I can't think we're right. Max Picard, who was a Swiss of all surprising things, said that they were a legitimate part of the human race and that there was never so much madness in the world as when Hitler put them all to death. It's not exactly logical, but I'm sure he was right. They look miserable to us because we put ourselves in their place and think how terrible we would feel if we were like them. But we're *not* like them, so how can we tell? Some of them may be unhappy, but we can't know enough about them to be able to judge the value of their lives to themselves. Mostly I think we are worried by the implication that our wonderful brains are not as absolutely infallible as we would like to think.'

'But still,' I said a little impatiently, 'you haven't told me why you think I was going to commit suicide. I still can think of no reason myself.'

'There wouldn't be a reason,' he replied, 'at least not a direct one. One of the mistakes people make is to regard suicide as a logical solution to a problem. You worry about your health or your job or your moral bankruptcy, whatever it is, and you say, "Suicide is the only answer", as if you were an adulterous ensign. But this isn't logical or rational. It's merely traditional. It's a word commonly thought of as a solution. If a child has to write an equation and can't work out the second half, he is apt to put " = 0" because he knows a lot of equations do end like that. It has a conventional look, and so does an overdose of sleeping-pills, but neither is more logical than putting out your eyes to stop reading Dickens.'

He bent his forehead forward to rest on his knees, then looked up again as if he were trying to come to a conclusion. Finally he said:

'I know what went wrong with you, but I don't know whether I can explain it to you. Let me try putting it this way.

'People not only have to be able to account for their surroundings and all the things that happen to them; they also have to be able to account for themselves. I don't mean they have to be self-conscious: on the contrary, self-consciousness is an inverted anxiety about outside things. But, apart from being this or that in relation to everything else, one is also just oneself, or, rather, one just *is*. You're not aware of it very often—at least, most people aren't—but it's nevertheless true, and also fairly obvious if you think of it. When we were crossing that last bit of the shelf just now I knew that if either of us slipped we'd be likely to go all the way, and I thought that if I saw you lying there dead it would mean a great many things to me—what to do, what to feel and so forth—but if I imagined myself instead it meant exactly nothing at all. "Me dead" in my own mind is an irrational phrase and can only make sense if I bring you or somebody else into it, like "When I'm dead don't bury me alone". Do you follow me so far?'

'Yes,' I said, 'but I'm not sure where we're going.'

'Alright,' he continued, 'if there were a third person here I could point to you and say, "He is alive, human, male, presumably mortal", and so forth and this would make sense between us.

But if I say to you "I am" it doesn't mean any more to you than if I said "Ooh" or "Ah". It's just an expletive, and yet it is true for me, and if you think a little you'll see that it's true for you, too.'

'Do you mean the fact that all the bits and pieces that make up the me that you know happen to be put together in this one particular whole?'

'No,' he replied, 'that's a good individualistic thought, but it's not the same as the simple fact that you are aware you are. It's knowledge, but it's entirely private and irrational. But to get on with the point: when a person's awareness of his own being is put in doubt he is in a much worse position than one who finds outside things too much for him, because there is no possible defence mechanism. And if the doubt goes on too long, then, as I say, he can no longer account for himself. He gets privately lost, and because he no longer has any reason to avoid danger or silly ideas he may easily kill himself. In a way this, too, is accidental, even though it looks planned, but it's different from the other cases because in fact he always destroys the last remnant of his own being before he actually dies. He denies himself.'

He laughed gently.

'I've never tried to put this into words before,' he said, 'and trying to communicate what is essentially irrational is extremely difficult, but I think that's the nearest I can get to it. I think that for some reason your hold on your own being had been weakened and you were not far short of saying "Oh well, that's done for", but unconsciously. This odd loss of memory about yourself bears me out. You haven't forgotten things outside yourself.'

He stretched his legs and then stiffly got to his feet.

'Before the sun goes,' he said, 'I think I will see if I can find some heather or bracken. There should be some about a thousand feet down, and we are going to be very cold like this. But if I don't find any in about twenty minutes I'll come back. I can't afford to miss the way, and it will get dark fairly quickly tonight.'

He stepped over the rocks and disappeared round the shoulder of the mountain.

Our eyrie faced about west. The wind seemed to be coming from there, though it was difficult to be sure because it broke up on the mountain face and went blustering round the rock until it could find its proper way again. Clouds were piling up over towards where I was facing, high cumulus far off, dark at the base and furred with wisps of white above, and closer at hand rippled blankets of grey creeping forward between the hills and mountains lower down. The sun was setting, not in glory but in bright defiance, driving yellow shafts through every gap between the clouds. Somewhere far beyond the storm it would soon be violet, red, and peaceful, telling the shepherds they could sleep at ease; but we were to watch the night warily.

'I am,' I said tentatively as I gazed. 'I am... I am...'

At first I knew what I was saying, repeating the sounds consciously as an experiment, like a baby toying with a new name. But soon I became aware that I was, and stopped saying anything. I just was. The hills and the clouds and the frustrated sun were no longer steep or grey or bright; they were a moving quietness, and what was quiet was me.

At last a flare of sunlight pierced low through the cloud and lit up, as it were in a frame, a small green patch far, far below me and away, with three white cottages and a dark line like a stream. People, I thought, and was half aware that the word was a disturbance, but the peace was undisturbed. Some other memory struggled for a hearing, but the sun was gone forever before I could recall it:

> And did the Countenance Divine
> Shine forth upon our clouded hills?
> And was Jerusalem builded here ...?

The spell went as the words came. Everything was darkening again in the west, and the cottages were invisible. I tried to recapture that sudden glimpse but could do no more than reaffirm that the lines I had remembered, surely out of a disused drawer, exactly conveyed it. Even they could not bring it back to life.

It was nearly night when he came back and put a clump of heather and bracken down beside me. He was a little out of breath.

'We want to get some of the heather under us,' he said, 'to keep us off the rock itself, and then we can use the rest for covering. It's not much, but it's better than nothing. I had to go further for it than I had expected. Have you been all right?'

We both set about making our beds and adding to the windbreak.

'Yes,' I said, 'I've been trying to see what you meant about being. I said "I am" a few times, and after a while I found that I was. But I've still no idea *who* I am.'

'Good Heavens!' he said, almost impatiently. 'What on earth do you want to know that for? *I'm* not interested. You'll spoil the whole thing if you go on worrying about second-hand things like that. It's for other people to fuss about what they call you and how they label and identify you. The only important thing for you is to be absolutely sure that you are. Don't even try to see yourself *as* anything. Just be.'

It was almost as if he were trying to save me from electrocuting myself, calling urgently, 'Don't touch it!' Then he relaxed and looked at me more mildly.

'Your memory will come back sooner or later, quite suddenly. Then you'll remember who you are and what role you have played in the world, that you can only recall now without yourself in it. But this doesn't matter. Whatever happened it obviously went wrong, and I hope that when it does come back it will be like a flat map and not real country, something you can recognise but not feel. Then, if only you can get some protection from the sort of attack that beat you last time, you'll be able to start again fresh and really live. But you haven't much time. You might remember tonight or tomorrow or any time.'

He chuckled.

'Come to think of it, a mountain isn't a bad place for making fresh starts. If we're to believe the story about Noah—and why shouldn't we?—the whole of life had to begin again from the top of Mount Ararat. It's a better story than the Greek one of Deucalion on Parnassus, which isn't much of a mountain. But think of Noah, six hundred and one years old and sitting eighteen thousand feet up on Ararat in charge of everything. He must have felt pretty strange, in spite of the promise he had from God. Once he got down everything was in good order again. Not perfect, because that was a word which hadn't been invented yet, but manageable—which, for some reason we're not told, it hadn't been before. And it still is manageable as long as you take it slowly and don't make mysteries where there are none. Anyway, Noah was so pleased with it that he planted a vineyard as quick as he could and got drunk. You'll be able to do the same with a clear conscience. You can do what you like once the anarchy has left your mind.'

That's as maybe, I thought, but the fact was that I had only been listening to him with half an ear. I had been wondering how to describe the scene of the sun shining on the cottages, the im-pression of which was still with me. Rather lamely I said:

'After you had gone for the heather there was a most extraordinary scene. The very last ray of sun hit a little group of cottages over there'—I pointed uselessly in the dark—'and for some reason it put me in mind of Blake's 'Jerusalem'. It was just as if a spotlight had picked out that one little place for special attention. My memory really must be quite good if I can remember poetry.'

He was quite still for a moment, but I thought I heard him draw in his breath sharply. Then he said:

'I suspect Blake had something rather larger in mind than a

cottage or two, but I suppose one never knows. Blake had a remarkable ability to make up unreal pictures that nevertheless rang true. Being and creation are like the opposite sides of the same coin, and poets have this gift of being able to turn the coin over a little so that they can get a glimpse at the other side. To some extent we are all poets if we try to be. We can, so to speak, disembody what we see, just as we can disembody ourselves for fractions of a second. But the real poet has the ability to take away his glimpses and re-embody them so that other people can see them, too.'

'But doesn't that apply to all artists?' I asked.

'I suppose so. But I like the word "poet" better. It has a more generous sound and it has been less damaged by abuse. Also I like to think of it in Greek, in its original sense. To them the poet was just the "maker", and their delicate minds stopped them from making him the maker of this or that. He wasn't limited or defined, like a cobbler or an actor, he was the purest kind of maker, composing harmonies of words which reminded them of the beauties they fleetingly descried but never tamed. He molded the quicksilver of splendour into songs they could sing. It just happened that the Greeks were better at words than anything else despite their being the best sculptors. But it doesn't matter what medium you use if you can capture beauty.' I heard him chuckle in the dark. 'What a thing it is! We all look for it like children look for the rainbow's end. It's useless, elusive, valueless, meaningless, and when we find it we're apt to treat it like a forbidden pet mouse and stuff it down into the corner of our minds. But we have to keep after it. Even poets can't capture it, but they snatch threads as it passes and use them to remind us.'

I said that I thought I saw what he meant, but he went on as if he had not heard me.

'Yes, these meaningless words, "being", "beauty", "poetry", are all very close to each other. Where one is the others are sure to be. We were talking about the vulnerability of people's being.

How do they become disintegrated? Abstraction, guilt, brutality. I think those are the right words.

'"Brutality" is fairly obvious. I don't mean cruelty or barbarity, but absolute insensitivity, which, oddly enough, seems to be a mark of high rather than low intelligence. Very simple people make up for their ignorance by a certain amount of what we call intuition; and they are intellectually humble, which really means that they leave what they don't understand to chance. Chance is very wise. They may be crude, but they're not often vicious. Jackals are always supposed to be very inferior animals, but in fact they only scrape their livelihood as best they can. But take the fox, who has been living next to civilisation. He really is vicious. He kills for fun. Compare the Germans and the Dyaks,[1] and I only use the Germans as an obvious example. This is a difficult championship to judge.'

Another long pause, and then:

'I shall have to take all that back, or most of it, to make my real point. Brutality is in fact only a form of abstraction, and as a matter of fact guilt is only one of its results. Do you remember anything about the war?'

I thought for a moment and then replied:

'Yes, but rather in the same way as I remember anything else. I can remember a lot of scenes and facts, but without myself being anywhere in them. I can remember London being bombed in September 1940, and Bayeux, and a place where there were a lot of Germans and cows all caught in the same enfilade from a naval pom-pom, and, I suppose, a lot of other things. But I'm always hidden somewhere behind the viewfinder. It's really as if I'd read about it, except that I have a feeling I was there.'

'You remember the mass raids on Germany?'

'Yes, but not at first hand. Not even behind the viewfinder.'

---

1   The Dyak or Dayak are one of the indigenous peoples of Borneo

'Well, think of this. If you were a bomber pilot, you went over and dropped your bombs, and you didn't think you were dropping them on marshalling-yards. As far as you were concerned this was the enemy and this was the best way of stopping him fighting. Look at the "the enemy" and the "him". If you thought about it afterwards, you might think that you, personally, had killed perhaps a thousand or more individual people, none of whom you could have identified as the enemy. You just wiped them out *en masse*. The same applies to the Germans who did the Coventry and Exeter raids. Now, I think that if you could go off and kill all those people at a distance, not knowing who they were and just thinking of them as "the enemy", you were being abstract. You were disposing of them as if they had no personal existence, and in fact whether you killed them or not was almost irrelevant.'

'But how can you wage war if people don't do that?' I asked. 'And surely a defensive war is justified?'

'You miss my point,' he said. 'I wish war didn't happen, at least on that scale. What I want you to see is that the pilot who said to himself: "I know there are a lot of miserable people who are going to suffer, and I hate to do it, but we've got to win and this is how we're told to do it"—that pilot is perhaps to be pitied because he has tried to recognise his victims. Certainly as a man he has nothing to blame himself for. But anyone who can say "This is war, and they're the enemy" deserves a quick death himself. He doesn't want to admit that people are people.'

I must have made some sound of incipient protest, because he immediately went on:

'No, don't think I'm a pacifist. I might be an objector, but in fact I have never seen a satisfactory answer to this particular problem. Not a general one, anyway. Take the other side of the picture. After the war it was popular to think that the Russians were a particularly nice people. They had done this and that on the credit side and therefore they were to be looked on as specifically nice. And this, if you know anything at all about Russia, is patent nonsense.

'Nowadays it's fashionable to be called a humanist, which as often as not means giving yourself an aura of virtue by affecting to love everyone. Generally it involves making pious statements about people of whom you know nothing at all. In any case, I think impersonal treatment of people, whether for good or for bad, is a dangerous abstraction. It's conceited and condescending. In war you should at least see the whites of their eyes, and in other times you should start your charity at home. You won't have enough of it to go far afield.'

The clouds I had been watching earlier in the distance had moved up to us, and the wind blew a sudden squall of rain which quite ignored the barriers which my companion had thought worthy the name of cave. We both flinched a little from it.

'We won't be able to do much more talking tonight,' he said, 'but to stop you getting the wrong impression from what I've been saying let me say this. I don't believe I am advocating any form of selfishness when I say that the most important thing is your own being. I do believe that "Thou shalt love thy neighbour as thyself", but I think this means that you have to start by loving yourself—valuing is perhaps better.'

The squall became an unremitting storm. Heather, bracken, wool and skin yielded successively before it, and in a brief lull after the first deep soaking my companion said:

'Face inwards and keep your back rounded, but if you have to move make sure I'm awake first, otherwise I might forget where I am and fall off. If you get very cold, try to think about your heart and all the warm blood pumping through it. Or try to think of nothing at all.'

For a while I lay curled up in a ball watching the storm envelop us through the back of my head. I wriggled so that my clothes stood a little away from my skin in as many places as possible and said to myself, 'Ha, ha, it's pouring down but it won't get through.'

And for a while it didn't get through but made my clothes feel warm and steamy like a hot towel such as barbers put very lightly round your face before they shave you. But I had been cold from the beginning. Lying out on the shelf in the afternoon had chilled me and I had done nothing since hard enough to restore my circulation. So the towel grew clammy and I had to shrink my skin further and further inwards to keep it clear. The wind dropped for a moment, and I felt a light pressure on the back of my neck.

'Wet wool is wind-proof,' said my companion, and as the rain came lashing in again I felt extraordinarily comforted.

But the comfort faded as the weather grew worse and worse. There must have been rank upon rank of those high grey clouds. I pictured them following each other smoothly across the sea and land, tall and frowning and wide about the hips like a procession of ill-tempered Queens from Wonderland shuffling toe to heel around the world. But I felt quite friendly towards them and did not blame them for my being cold.

Thinking about your heart really is quite effective if you can concentrate on it. You see a great red bellows pumping safely away at a temperature of 98.4 degrees Fahrenheit and after a while there are moments when you think you are looking into a firebox. But it is difficult to concentrate for long.

I also tried to think about what my companion had been saying. At the time I had thought he was probably right, though it needed some reflection, but I found that I could not piece it all together again. I thought I had seen what he meant when he used the word "being", and the notion that beauty was useless gave me a little thrill of pleasure, but I could not reconstruct more and eventually I fell asleep.

Although the cold and rain constantly woke me and made me try to wriggle myself free of my sodden clothes and to keep still at all costs and not shiver, I was hardly aware of having been conscious for much of the night when my companion nudged me. The wind had dropped and changed, and our side of the mountain was nearly still. The first light had just managed to prevail over the storm-laden eastern sky, and I could make out that rain was still falling. But our overhang was protecting us now that we had survived without it. It would not have been possible to be wetter if we had been pulled out of a river, and for the first time I felt extremely hungry.

'We'd better start as soon as we can see where we're going,' he said. 'That'll be in about twenty minutes, I hope. Take your boots and stockings right off and I'll try and rub some circulation back into your legs. You can do mine. If we don't, we'll fall at the first bad foot-hold. How's your ankle?'

I felt it. I had loosened the laces of my boots before we settled down and my stockings had been soaked right through, and this seemed to have had the effect of a cold compress, because although the ankle was still sore it was not nearly as swollen as it had been. I told him it seemed to be better.

'Good,' he said as he finished taking off his own boots. 'It's going to be an interesting journey for you, and it would be a pity if it were spoilt by having to think about a mere ankle. Pain is useful enough as a reminder or a warning, but it's an awful nuisance as a distraction. Have you remembered who you are yet?'

'No,' I said, 'I haven't really thought about it anymore.'

I suddenly realised that, indeed, I hadn't even wondered.

'Good again,' he said. 'I told you already your memory would come back all too soon.'

'It's odd', I said, 'to have a part of you that goes on and off work when it chooses.'

'No more odd that your memory should do that than the rest of your brain when you go to sleep. Or for that matter a muscle that's over-tired.'

'I suppose it's subconscious.'

'If you like. You're not aware of it at the time, so I suppose it's true to say it's subconscious. But don't for pity's sake imagine that there's some sort of independent force in you called *the* Subconscious. For that matter, it's also involuntary, but that doesn't mean there's a piece of you called your Will that actually decides to do things. There are just varying degrees and patterns of consciousness. All these mystical nouns made by putting a definite article in front of an adjective or a verb and imagining that that necessarily creates a Thing are the most dangerous form of abstraction. Learn to be content that you are; that is the first truth. Remind yourself always that the intangibles that you perceive when you are most conscious of being are the first realities. God, wonder, beauty, love, generosity—a mixed bag, but that's the fault of the language they are put into. They are still the elements of life. Everything else can be coped with more or less mechanically through your nervous system, and you can be sure of that to the extent that you can be sure of the system. But it's just as difficult to be as sure of it as of being. Shun the abstract bogeys like the plague. Good, Evil, Perfection, Sin and all the rest. They're the only excuse I know for believing in devils.'

'But surely,' I said, 'conversation would be difficult without them?'

'Oh, yes,' he replied calmly, 'conversation certainly would be difficult, and I have no objection to people inventing all the words they need. All the fun in talking and speculation comes from seeing whether you can fit words in to fill gaps in your knowledge. But people get into bad habits. They turn words into things; they pretend they're sticks and beat people with them; and when a word has acquired enough status it actually has the power to hurt.

'A long time ago someone looked at a volcano and said, "Because fire is coming out of that mountain there must be something inside." Someone else then said, "The thing inside is called a dragon", and everyone agreed that this was a delightful way of filling the unknown. So now the English revere a Thracian who killed some dragon that had presumably grown tired of its mountain, while millions of others are genuinely terrified by a creature that doesn't exist.'

He laughed.

'Still,' he went on, 'dragons are almost beneficent compared with the really miasmic words. Good and Evil are my pet aversions because so many of the others stem from them. Originally, people said things were good when they pleased them and bad when they didn't. It was a matter of individual taste. The fact that some things called pain displease nearly everyone doesn't make *a thing* of pain. If there is some substance called the Good in chocolate, which pleases a lot of people, why doesn't it please everyone? If you agree that God is good, how can there be an opposite, and what can any of those millions of people down there tell us about God or Good? Has someone poked his head down the volcano and pulled out a dragon? Give me a poet any day, who can put me in mind of God and beauty without trying to persuade me of a lot of abstract horrors.

'Come on. We'd better be on our way. It will take us quite a while to get down.'

As we were getting to our feet I asked him:

'But isn't "beauty" an abstract word?'

'Technically, I suppose it is,' he replied, 'but in fact it's really another expletive. It doesn't have much of a dictionary meaning that tells you anything about it. Men are all pretty alike, you know, and over the ages a good deal of our conversation has been devoted to trying to share our intangible enjoyments. So a few words have crept in among the practical ones which are simply our best attempt at expressing the inexpressible. But they've been badly battered by those who think Man lives by words alone provided they have meanings.'

We started slowly along a sheep-track that followed the contour, barely three hundred feet below the summit, which now appeared at intervals through rifts in the cloud. I realised that the things he was saying were still largely escaping me. The words were all right; I could understand them well enough; but I found it difficult to keep continuity, so that the whole somewhat resembled a melody played staccato very slowly. It was difficult to remember the beginning by the time I had got to the end. In the ordinary way, talk of this kind impinges on thousands of wishes, needs, prejudices and habits of thought which have been collected as by-products of things suffered and enjoyed, of questions asked and answered. There is a further layer of vicarious or generalized knowledge, but on the whole new ideas must pass through the test of what is directly known. A word like 'sin' is first referred to actual guilts and accusations; 'good' is referred to an immediately recent pleasure. But I had nothing of my own to refer to. I knew what he was talking about in that I knew the meanings of the sentences, but I could not connect them with my own experience and they therefore failed to hold my attention. Moral philosophy hardly takes root where fear is absent and the conscience clear. Mine was empty, which came to the same thing.

We had gone barely a hundred yards when I realised that he had been right in forecasting slow progress. Already my ankle had started to swell again, and I asked him to stop so that I could loosen the laces. He sat down beside me as if we had all day for our descent—which, indeed, I supposed we had.

'You remember the story of the Garden of Eden?' he asked me.

'Yes.'

'And the famous tree?'

'Yes.'

'Can you explain to me why people always seem to think that it was the tree of good and evil, when it was actually the tree of the *knowledge* of good and evil?'

'I don't remember ever having thought much about it. Surely it's one of those fables that one's taught when young and then forgets.'

'Oh, I think it's probably a fable all right, though it's difficult to be dogmatic at such a distance. Giving two different accounts of the Creation doesn't inspire one to take either literally. But so much has been made of that tree. We are supposed because of it to believe that an absolute power of evil exists, which has led to the Devil and Hell and all the other paraphernalia that have been used for burning witches and intimidating and blackmailing the young and the ignorant. But I like to suppose that it meant roughly what it said: that when people start *knowing about* Good and Evil instead of saying that this or that for them is good or evil, then they are cut off from the tree of life, which is what happened to Adam. I think it was a warning against being dogmatic about ultimate values, and particularly against judging people as if one were God.'

'But surely', I ventured, 'you are going against rather a long and respectable line of thought, aren't you?'

'I'm afraid so,' he answered equably, 'but I'm not the first and anyway, lineage is not always the best criterion. As for respectability, the Devil has been believed in by some people in the best of faith, but he's also been used for the nastiest crimes. Tyrants have always liked to have theological backing, and a lot of them have become tyrants by being too fanatical about some dogma. Believe me, philosophers and theologians have been among the greatest enemies of truth because they so often try to get too far in order simply to be right. It is difficult to be pure in heart if you have a lot of dogmatic axes to grind.'

The cloud was gradually lifting and, although from time to time a low-hanging wisp would blot us out from the world below, we could watch the weak light gradually creep down the hills opposite until they were all grey and the valleys black chasms running through them. A little life was astir, too, which I had not seen in the evening. Some wild duck flew fast to the west to some water I could not see; a pair of swans went past so far below us that we could hardly see them, but making with their wings the first live noise we had heard other than our voices; a pair of hooded crows alighted wickedly on the hillside opposite. I did not feel quite the tranquillity of the previous evening, when the world had been withdrawing against the rainy night, but a warmth like love, and a wondering expectancy such as one has on opening a well-packed parcel. Look at it all, I said to myself; and here I am. Where can I begin? And because I could not take my eyes off it I suffered more than I need have done as we walked the next stretch.

When we sat down again my companion said:

'I'm a bit warmer now. I hope you are, too. Have you realised what an extraordinary day you're starting?'

'No,' I said, 'I hadn't thought about it.'

He looked at me quizzically.

'Well, do so,' he said with a laugh, 'or you'll miss a very rare experience.'

'I suppose it is going to be a bit strange getting down among people again and not having the remotest idea who I am or who I know or where I live. But up here it doesn't seem to matter too much.'

'Nor does it matter, but that's not the point I have in mind. I expect a great many people recover a lost memory every day. There's nothing very unusual in that. You've done something quite different. Yesterday you were in despair, you were lost. You probably hadn't decided to do away with yourself, but you'd been done away with. We don't know how, but that doesn't matter. But today, lost memory and all, you look at the world you'd given up as if it was your most precious possession. And that after as wet a night as I've ever experienced.'

'But', I said, suddenly feeling hollow in my diaphragm, 'when my memory comes back—and you say it will—presumably all the things which you say drove me to suicide will come back again. So I might as well turn right round now.'

I felt as I said it that the last sentence was stupid and even in rather bad taste, but he seemed to ignore it. At least there was no trace of displeasure in his voice when he replied; rather, it seemed as if his eagerness was mounting.

'No,' he said, 'I don't think that is likely to happen. You have to see yourself like a citadel besieged by demons. Demons aren't true, but all the bad intelligence you have been given leads you to think they are. In the end you get to the point where you will blow yourself up rather than surrender alive to the horrors which you can now practically see outside your walls. Do you follow me?'

I nodded, although he was not looking at me.

'Well, I believe that this night out on the mountain will have shown you that demons aren't true, and, if that's so, there's nothing to worry about. That's what made me think of Noah last night. But he had to wait a hundred and ninety days while the world was washed and rinsed and dried out again so that it was fit to live in. You've only had to wait a night.'

'What makes you so sure that my demons aren't real?'

'Because they only exist in your brain. They are the way you have learned to look at things, the associations you have built up and had built up for you. You know white is white, but if you are told too often and too compellingly that it's black you'll end up with your brain reacting to it as if it *was* black. You will abdicate. People call this brain-washing nowadays, because a certain form of it has been popularised, but in a subtler way it goes on the whole time. People try to persuade you that this or that is right or wrong, or that such and such is true or false. Generally it's harmless enough, but very often the reason behind it is this terrible insufficiency that drives people to boss each other about. It's to my mind a worse form of outrage than straightforward killing.'

'It would be a bit difficult to teach anyone anything at all if one were to take you literally. Someone has to do some telling.'

'I agree it's difficult to know where to draw the line, but I think there is a good test. Does the persuader hold his victim in contempt or not? Does he despise him, does he think him inferior, or even that he has no right to exist? Does he even know he exists? Of course it by no means goes without saying that he's bound to succeed. Some people have such a strong foundation in their own being that they can resist. But it doesn't alter the offence.

'I've often wondered how it came about that nearly all the poets in Russia committed suicide sooner or later after the Revolution. Pasternak was the chief exception, but he must have been an exceptionally strong character and a few centuries of the ghetto breed toughness. Most of them were more or less on the side of the Revolution, and if its savagery shocked them its hard-ship was not likely to do so. Even the stupidity of all the big and little tyrants who sprang up was hardly a cause for suicide. And yet they did it.

'Remember they were poets, some of them even good ones. They woke up to the fact that the new czars were Marxists and that for Marxists people have the same kind of value as cows. They're economic units. Personal units are dangerous, and poets are contemptible and subversive. All this is the opposite to what they have thought. But in course of time, if you live in a really well-run tyranny like that, you begin to have doubts about yourself. Because you can't say what you think, your power to think gets rusty. And the more the material success and the torrents of words overwhelm you the more your little self becomes weakened, until at last it turns at bay and puts an end to its own integrity.'

He kicked angrily at a small rock.

'Why did the Russians of all people get caught by Marxism?' he asked. 'They used to have more poetic sense than most, and they had that eccentricity which is always a sign that persons are conceded to be persons. If I was taken back sixty years or so and asked to prophesy who would be Christian and who Marxist, I should have said that the Russians would be Christian, the

English, Swedes and Swiss Marxist and the Americans half and half. Perhaps I'm only wrong on my timing after all. Certainly the sombre pharisaical certainties of Marx and Lenin seem to be better suited to industrialists and bankers and the humble liberalities of Jesus to the prodigals who made Russian literature. It's one of history's perversities.'

With that he stood up again and made off downhill with me stumbling in his wake. I had still hardly looked at his face, and even now I think of him in terms of his back view if I try to visualise him. For that matter, he hardly looked at me, staring at his toes or off into the distance most of the time and only suddenly turning to me if he had a new idea or if he wanted to emphasise something. And then he looked at me quite without curiosity, as if he had known me all my life. At one point I even found myself wondering whether he was an old friend, but from the way he talked this seemed impossible, and so he remained for me an indeterminate man seen from the back, dressed in indeterminate tweed made even more so by its wetness.

We had gone perhaps another five hundred yards, and I was beginning to feel that I had done as much as I could, when a hanging cloud enveloped us and my companion called a halt.

'It's not worth missing the easy way,' he said. 'You wouldn't thank me if we had to go further than we need, and still less if we started having to walk like goats.'

'You may think it funny,' I said, 'but it hadn't occurred to me to thank you. I suppose it should, but it didn't. But you can be sure I shan't blame you.'

'That's good,' he said cheerfully. 'Blaming is only a way of making oneself feel better by making someone else feel worse. But people are always doing it.'

'Wouldn't you blame me if I tried to kill you?' I asked.

'What a question!' he laughed. 'But I don't think I would. I'd try to stop you, and I might even think it was necessary for you to be locked up so that you couldn't try again. But I wouldn't blame you in the sense of making a definitive and unfavourable judgement on your entire person. I already think you are wrong in one respect: you are trying to use a purely hypothetical situation in order to form a principle. At least, I hope it's hypothetical.'

'Oh, I think I'm safe enough,' I said, though I thought to myself that perhaps I wasn't if the truth were known. 'But I don't follow you.'

'People who are always imagining situations tend to look for abstract principles. They come out with statements like "Anyone who can do that ought to be shot", or they read cases in the paper and form judgements which are not their business. They even kill on principle. I can understand someone committing murder out of temper or exasperation or in self-defence, but I could never sit on a jury and sentence a man to death simply because the principle of the law says so. The smugness of juries is something I imagine myself, and that is why I just said what I did, but in fact I don't know what I could do and I don't intend to worry about it until I have to. But if I had to give an answer one way or the other in the abstract, that would be it.'

'But how would laws ever be made if people didn't suppose situations? I thought it was one's duty as a citizen to argue about these things.'

'Good laws are based on facts, not on principles. Life would be much easier and freer if there weren't so many so-called good citizens minding other people's business, or even fictitious business, and making them vote for laws they can't possibly understand.'

He said this rather shortly and apparently regretted it.

'What I really mean', he went on less vehemently, 'is that laws are purely social things. You have to have them or you couldn't maintain society. But they have no importance in relation to the ultimate value of a person. A criminal may go to prison, but no one can have the right to consider him, as it were, a non-person.

It's the sanctimoniousness of good citizens that annoys me. They try to make absolute morality out of what is just practical politics. But to get back to hypotheses, don't they tend to substitute the possible for the actual?'

'Surely you must reckon with possibilities?'

'With probabilities up to a point, I agree, but possibilities are only those things which either didn't happen or might not happen. They're too vague to worry about.'

'What about our own choice in the matter?'

'What choice?' He looked up as if genuinely astonished. 'I don't see that we have any choice in what happens. Mind you, I don't believe in hopeless predestination, either. We do more than just be happened to, and I've no use for the supposedly oriental idea that you should just sit there and take it. I wonder if in fact Orientals believe quite that. But the notion that everything is just ready to happen and then something called our free-will gives us a little shove this way or that seems to me quite gratuitous. I even suspect it's demonstrably not so. Of course, as long as you believe in absolute Evil you have to invent free-will so that you can blame people for preferring the Devil and so put yourself in the right with God. It's just arrogance and narrow-mindedness, and I doubt whether it's greatly appreciated. Do you think people actually say, "Now I know your plans I'll think them over, but if they don't suit me I'll go my own way"? It's almost blasphemous to suggest it. And if they don't believe in God all they can have is the conceit that they are doing what they want, which is a tautology.'

'Do you believe in God?' I asked, wishing I hadn't.

'No,' he answered in a matter-of-fact way. 'I think I know him a little. I used the word "believe" because it's the usual one, but I think it gives rise to terrible misunderstanding. To me it's something I know—that's the wrong word, too—something I am aware of like I'm aware of being, stronger than knowing. It's a question of poetry again, nothing that I can explain rationally. So-called proofs of God and all the talk and writing that goes on are really self-contradictory, though the best of it has a certain poetry that I understand. In the long run, though, I have just to sit quietly and stop arguing, as you sit under a summer sky. Then I can consent to everything without any violence to my reason.'

He turned and gave me a quick glance, and there was a certain gaiety in his eyes that told me that this was an idea which pleased him.

'Yes,' he went on emphatically as he gazed out into space again, 'that's the best word I can find consent. I don't mean it in the permissive sense. I don't feel "if that's the way things are I'd better agree to it". I feel that I can live along with everything else. "There's the world," I say, "and there's me in the middle of it, and the more I can know about it and the more I can be myself at the same time the happier I am." Do you see what I mean?'

'I think so,' I said. 'You mean you take part in it all.'

'That's it. What I know about that's outside me I accept inside. I go along with it. But this has nothing to do with passiveness or withdrawal; on the contrary, it implies a conscious act of being aware—as aware as possible. I think that sometimes this is what is meant when people talk about free-will. "Thy will be done" is desire, not resignation. And of course there is an alternative attitude: that of not being aware and not accepting, of hustling events or complaining about them. But I still don't think that anyone has an option between the two. Everyone in fact does a little of each.'

'It certainly sounds like a doctrine of perfection,' I said.

'It's not a doctrine,' he retorted. 'It's just the way I happen to see things. A doctrine of perfection is bound to lead to grief, because no one can imitate God. As long as we have this dualism about us there's bound to be conflict between the excitable electro-chemical device on the one hand and the unique being on the other, and between the soloist and the second from the left in the back row of the choir. The great thing is to make the best of it both ways. Why science and religion must always be at loggerheads is quite beyond me. Jealousy, aided by moral rectitude and nourished on the fruit of that awful tree.'

The cloud was beginning to thin. It drifted across us in patches, and each dark patch became successively smaller and the light ones lighter. My companion sighed and said wistfully:

'It's funny that I should be so certain that what I've been telling you is true and yet I cannot let my own life follow it. I suppose my brain has been too cluttered up with other people's views. It's like having your eyesight but being kept in a dark room. But perhaps you could manage better, starting from the beginning again. If you remember that the most important thing about you is that you are, that it is your own being that sees beauty and the reflection of God, you'll be able to live with life instead of arguing with it. But don't let people bribe and blackmail you into parting with yourself. They'll try. They'll put smoke into your fresh air and they'll try to put a ceiling over you instead of the sky. Don't let them. There will always be enough who'll leave you in peace.'

The last of the cloud blew away and, like a veil removed, revealed that the dull world we had last looked at was now an array of colour under a cloudless sky made golden by the morning sun. The storm had rolled away behind us, out of sight on the other side of the mountain. The view filled me with a new zest. I wanted to play with the world, to walk about it and handle it. There it was below me, limitless fields and mountains and beyond them seas and deserts, rivers and forests, villages and cities. I had no sense of possession, no wish to own them or rule them or change them. I wanted to walk all over the world unnoticed, observing and enjoying but not interfering. But first I must get down.

I got to my feet with something of a scramble as my companion did the same more composedly. I found him looking at me with a warmth that he had not shown before.

'Yes, we'd better move,' he said, and then, as if he had been reading my thoughts: 'It's a wonderful sight, isn't it? Don't you feel you would like it all for your private garden, to come and go in as you like? The rain has washed it clean and the sun has warmed it, and you could stroll in it for the rest of your life.'

Until now he had walked ahead of me, but now he waited for me to come up with him and walked beside me.

'But I'm afraid you can't,' he said. 'Even Noah had to remember that the world is a practical affair, full of laws and problems and the need to be busy. Once you get down there you'll be more strolled upon than strolling.'

I must have unconsciously shown disappointment or disbelief, for he went on:

'You can't get away from the fact that you've got to eat and keep warm and get on with other people in order to survive. It's no use thinking of the hermit's life. That's just running away. Most of the mystical ways involve diminishing life as far as possible, which means getting as near death as you can, and I think you've had enough of that. You'll die in due course, and meanwhile the problem is to live. You'll find you have a past, which will tie you down somewhat; and you'll start again at one particular time and place, which will also limit your freedom. Don't, incidentally, imagine you have any freedom apart from your partial detachment from reason; it's a word that's generally used as a protest against the obvious fact that it's at best a very relative affair. Imagine all the things that will happen to you without any by-your-leave, yet you'll have to respond to them somehow or other. That's what life is, and it's into life that you are very shortly going to be decanted. But remember that it is *you* who have been inserted into this enormous mechanism. And the mechanism works. Most of the fun is in finding out how it works, but don't worry about why it works or complain that it does work in that particular way. There's nothing you can do to change it.'

'It can't be improved?'

'No, it can't,' he answered with some vehemence. 'It changes the whole time, and some people think they can see an improvement, but it's only from their limited point of view. You'll find plenty of zealous reformers, but beware of them. You may even think one day that you've made an improvement. Put it aside. You may be an agent of some change but never either an in-novator or an improver. If there is ever Paradise on earth, which I don't anticipate, it won't be due to local reforms. The only paradise I can imagine is one where everyone lives quietly, paying no more heed than they have to the works of Man and as much as they can to those of God, and, above all, respecting each other's idiocy.'

He glanced around, then stopped in his tracks and pointed eagerly to a rainbow curved over the summit we had left.

'I don't seem to be able to get away from Noah,' he said. 'In fact I'm no longer inclined to believe he was only a legend. Do you remember that the sign God gave him that there would not be another flood was a rainbow? I particularly like that part of the story. The token was beautiful and intangible. Men were licensed to be poets by it as well as to live on dry land.'

We watched the rainbow for a while and then resumed our march downward.

'Always look at rainbows,' he said after we had gone some way. 'Don't analyse them into light and raindrops. That was interesting when it was first realised, but it isn't now. Just look and realise how beautiful they are, especially the ones that are made by little clouds passing over the moon just before dawn.'

We continued downwards in silence until after a few minutes we had to climb again to cross an intermediary ridge which lay between our mountain and the valley. We went slowly and often halted, because my ankle was only just able to support me, but we said no more until we reached the top of the ridge. There we let ourselves drop in a clump of heather. I took my left boot off and uselessly fingered the swelling, feeling that I had gone as far as I could. My companion lay with his chin cupped in his hands and scanned the long easy slope ahead which led straight to the valley and the road.

Soon he said:

'Look down there. That must be a search-party. Somebody must have noticed you yesterday after all, though they seem to have taken their time worrying about you.'

Far away on the brown beginning of the hillside could be seen a line of five men. I could just see that they swayed slightly from side to side, and this showed that they were climbing towards us. They had nearly two miles to come.

'In that case there's no need for me to stay,' he went on. 'I've a long way to go, and in the opposite direction. If I were you, I'd wait here. They'll be able to help you down between them and save that ankle of yours. You won't think I'm deserting you?'

I was so taken aback that I could not answer at once. His presence was the only furniture I had in my new condition, and the patient persistent voice had become for me what the sound of the breakers is to a dweller on the seashore. Even when he was not talking there was an undertone of suspended words, like the faint swishing of the lapping wavelets on a calm day. If he went, the whole of my experience would go with him. It is difficult to recall this predicament fully in retrospect, but it was as if I was destined to lose my memory again and with it my existence in the world.

My first reasonable thought was that he had said 'in the opposite direction' and that this held only a little glen which led to the top of the next ridge to the west and over that to the endless sea of hills I had been looking at last night. The only sign of human dwelling I had seen there was the little group of buildings that had been lit up briefly as the sun went down, and that must have been nearly ten miles away by foot. If he were going there, surely there would be a road skirting nearer to the south? It struck me for a moment that he might be a fugitive, but it was obvious that in that case he would not have risked his safety for so long escorting a lame man back to what would be the opposite of safety to him. Besides, it was impossible to attribute anything so devious and turbulent to someone who in every way conveyed simplicity and calm. Yet I could not bring myself to ask him where he was going. The way in which he had said, 'I've a long way to go, and in the opposite direction', with a little pause for clarity where I have put the comma, made it clear that this was sufficient information for my needs and an adequate explanation.

'I don't really know,' I said at last. 'It seems odd, after all these hours, that you should suddenly fade away, here and now, in the middle of nowhere. After all, you're the only thing I remember about myself.'

He smiled and said:

'I don't think that will last long, and the fact is I cannot be of any use to you now. You've got to get down again'—he hesitated and smiled—'to plant your vineyard and drink your wine, and those people will manage very well without me. I've nothing particular to say to them and I must go as soon as I can.'

He was on his feet, and I noticed that he took care to stand just below the sky-line, out of sight of the approaching searchers. Again I wondered whether he was afraid of them and again I saw how absurd the thought was. More probably he was anxious to avoid embarrassment.

'At least I should say thank you,' I said, 'though it sounds rather weak.'

'No, don't on any account do that,' he said sharply. 'To say thank you is a civility which is useful to bridge the gulf between people, to reassure them. But I don't need reassuring, and we haven't built any gulf between us. Perhaps that's because I've done all the talking and we haven't been able to argue. Do not try to feel gratitude, which has all the vices of a promissory note.

Just accept everyone for what he is, and when he does you good be glad, and when he does you harm be sorry. But neither tie yourself to him with gratitude nor make yourself responsible for him by judgement.'

He held out his hand, but as if he neither wanted nor had the habit of it. I did the same, as awkwardly, and our handshake was perfunctory and uncommunicative.

'Anyway,' he said, 'I hope you remember to look at rainbows.' And he walked quickly away.

He was out of sight at once round a shoulder, and I turned my attention to the distant search-party. The air was quite clear, as it often is in the hills after rain, and after I had been looking for a while I thought that I could make out that one of the men was in blue police uniform. Certainly his clothes were darker than the others, and he had a squared-off line to the top of his head which made a marked contrast to the blurred finish of his neighbours. Again I thought: Can it be true that he's on the run? And this time I slipped backwards down the slope and round the corner where he had gone. But he was already far away. I called as loudly as I dared and he heard me, but he only turned, waved, and continued on his way, moving fast. There was nothing I could do to warn or reassure him, so I climbed back to the ridge and resolved that I would not say I had seen him.

I've always wondered who he was, but I've never found out. He just appeared and disappeared.

卌

Christopher Burney (1917 – 1980) was a descendant of the prominent Scots Burneys. He was born in India, educated in England (at Wellington College before he ran away) and married to a Scots girl, Julia Burrell. Burney fought for The South Wales Borderers in the Narvik campaign of 1940 before joining a newly formed Commando unit. He left for the Special Operations Executive (SOE) in 1942 and was dropped into France as an enemy agent. He was captured after eleven weeks, interrogated under torture and then dispatched to Fresnes gaol outside Paris where he spent eighteen months in solitary confinement. In January 1944 he was sent to Buchenwald concentration camp in Germany. He survived and was liberated in April 1945. He wrote two books about his experiences, *Solitary Confinement* (1952 and 1961) and *Dungeon Democracy* (1946). In 1962 he published an allegorical story *Descent from Ararat* about his post traumatic stress. He died in 1970, survived by Julia and their two children.

Ted Gioia is a music historian and the author of eleven books, including *Music: A Subversive History* and *How to Listen to Jazz*. Three of his books—*Work Songs, Healing Songs, and Love Songs*—have each been honored with the ASCAP Deems Taylor/Virgil Thomson Award. Gioia's wide-ranging activities as a critic, scholar, performer, and educator have established him as a leading global guide to music past, present, and future.

Hugh Purcell was a BBC producer first in radio then in television between 1968 and 1994 specialising in history programmes. Prominent among them was an eight-part TV series *The Roads to War* that took a country-by-country approach to the causes of World War Two and then a five-part TV series *Living Islam* about what it means to be a Muslim in Britain today. He left to teach film, in Denmark, Cuba and India before changing to his second career as a writer. He has written biographies of little-known 20th century figures who deserve to be of national importance. The first was Tom Wintringham (*The Last English Revolutionary*) and the third is Christopher Burney (*Tragic Heroes: The Burney Brothers of Hay at War*).

‖‖

Other Titles in the Recovered Books series from Boiler House Press

Gentleman Overboard by Herbert Clyde Lewis
Introduction by George Szirtes, Afterword by Brad Bigelow
ISBN: 9781913861230

Pull Devil, Pull Baker by Stella Benson
Introduction by Julia Blackburn, Afterword by Nicola Darwood
ISBN: 9781913861605

Time: the Present – Selected Stories by Tess Slesinger
Introduction by Vivian Gornick, Afterword by Paula Rabinowitz
ISBN: 9781913861582

Two Thousand Million Man-Power by Gertrude Trevelyan
Introduction by Rachel Hore, Afterword by Brad Bigelow
ISBN: 9781913861858

Quarry by Jane White
Introduction by Anne Billson, Afterword by Helen Hughes
ISBN: 9781915812001

The Sanity Inspectors by Friedrich Deich
Introduction by Sinclair McKay, Afterword by Chris Maloney
ISBN: 9781913861872

To Test the Joy: Selected Poetry and Prose by Genevieve Taggard
Introduction by Terese Svoboda, Edited and with commentary
by Anne Hammond
ISBN: 9781915812025

William's Wife by Gertrude Trevelyan
Introduction by Alice Jolly, Afterword by Anne Kennedy Smith
ISBN: 9781915812063

Time Stood Still by Paul Cohen-Portheim
Introduction by Andrea Pitzer, Afterword by Panikos Panayi
ISBN: 9781915812056

No More Giant by Joaquina Ballard Howles
Introduction by Judy Blunt, Afterword by Nancy Cook
ISBN: 9781915812094

Mortal Leap by MacDonald Harris
Introduction by Jonathan Coe, Afterword by Steven G. Kellman
ISBN: 9781915812100

As It Was in the Beginning by Gertrude Trevelyan
Introduction by Kim Adrian, Afterword by Stanislava Dikova
ISBN: 9781913861582

The Bitter Roots by Norman Macleod
Introduction by Joanna Pocock, Afterword by Gabriella Graceffo
ISBN: 978191915812384

Red House Alley by Else Jerusalem
Introduction by Sophie Haydock, Afterword by Stephanie G. Ortega
Translated by Stephanie G. Ortega
ISBN: 9781915812360

Solitary Confinement
By Christopher Burney

First published in this edition by Boiler House Press, 2025
Boiler House Press is part of the UEA Publishing Project
Solitary Confinement copyright © Christopher Burney,
1951 and 1962
Descent from Ararat copright © Christopher Burney 1962, 1980.
Introduction copyright © Ted Gioia, 2025
Afterword copyright © Hugh Purcell, 2025

Photographs of Christopher Burney courtesy of Juliette Paton.

The right of Christopher Burney to be identified as the Author of
this work has been asserted by him in accordance with the Copyright, Design & Patents Act, 1988.

Proofreading by Alexandra Seale

Cover Design and Typesetting by Louise Aspinall
Typeset in Arnhem Pro

ISBN: 978-1-915812-46-9

9 781915 812469